the Maker's guide to Cricut

Easy Projects for Creating Fabulous Home Decor, Wearables, and Gifts

The Maker's Guide to Cricut:

Easy Projects for Creating Fabulous Home Decor, Wearables, and Gifts

Megan Meketa

Editor: Kelly Reed
Project manager: Lisa Brazieal
Marketing coordinator: Katie Walker
Copyeditor: Joan Dixon
Proofreader: Patricia J Pane
Interior layout: Danielle Foster
Cover design: Aren Straiger
Cover photograph: Megan Meketa

ISBN: 978-1-68198-833-7
1st Edition (1st printing, November 2023)
© 2022 Megan Meketa
All photographs © Megan Meketa

Rocky Nook Inc.
1010 B Street, Suite 350
San Rafael, CA 94901
USA

www.rockynook.com

Distributed in the UK and Europe by Publishers Group UK
Distributed in the U.S. and all other territories by Ingram Publisher Services

Library of Congress Control Number: 2021944857

This book is printed on acid-free paper.
Printed in China.

the Maker's guide to Cricut

Easy Projects for Creating Fabulous Home Decor, Wearables, and Gifts

MEGAN MEKETA
of Lovebird Heartworks

Table of Contents

Introduction

Reads as cry-cut, sounds like cricket. Cricut brand electronic cutting machines can be life-changing, let me tell you! What might start out as a fun pastime of cutting vinyl decals, creating cards, customizing shirts, and making custom labels around your home can quickly become a passionate hobby or can turn into a small business. My point being, a Cricut machine and its possibilities can be whatever you want it to be. Get creative, explore your machine and the software, and let's get making!

WHAT IS CRICUT?

There are several Cricut models to choose from. The No. 1 question I am asked is, "Which machine should I buy?" My answer is, "If you could dream up what you would like to create in the next several months to a year, what would you include?" Check out the machines listed below to help narrow down your choice.

CRICUT JOY The smallest of the Cricut cutting machines. This little cutie is a whiz when it comes to making custom cards, but the Joy can do so much more. This machine can cut a wide variety of materials including cardstock, vinyl, iron-on, sticker paper, cardboard, and faux leather; and it can even cut lengths up to 20 feet long (of a repeated cut/pattern) when using Cricut Smart Materials. The Joy can also electronically write, which is a great option for making labels, cards, envelopes, and more. However, there are limits to Joy's capabilities. The compatible materials list for the Cricut Joy is shorter than the other machines and there is no option for Print Then Cut, which is important to know if you plan on making stickers. Cricut Joy Smart Vinyl is 5.5″ wide and the maximum cut width is 4.5″ if using a Cricut Joy Mat.

CRICUT EXPLORE (AIR) SERIES These machines are full size and can cut more than 100 different types of materials. The Explore Air machines are a great option if you want to mainly work with cardstock, stickers, leather, vinyl, and iron-on materials. There is a blade for bonded fabric as well as a Deep-Point Blade that is compatible with this machine. The Explore machines have a dual tool holder, which means your machine can hold a Fine-Point Blade and a Scoring Tool or a pen at the same time. This machine can cut material up to 2mm thick. The dial on the Air and Air 2 machines only mentions some of the materials you can cut with these machines, but you can select the Custom option from the dial and it opens up a list with many more options when it comes time to Make It. The Air 3 model does not have a dial, but you will select your material from a list within Cricut Design Space. Unlike the first two versions of the Explore machines, the Air 3 is capable of cutting Smart Vinyl without a mat for cuts/designs larger than 11.5″ × 23.5″, which is the maximum size of the previous Explore machines.

CRICUT MAKER This machine is the cream of the crop! It has all the features of the other machines and more. My favorite things about this machine that the others don't have are the blades and specialty tools for cutting more than 300 types of materials. Many of these tools are used for the projects within this book, like the Rotary Blade for cutting felt and the Knife Blade for cutting craft foam. While the Explore Air 2 has blades that will work for felt and foam, I've found the Maker delivers the smoothest results (more on that when we get to those projects). Other than the blades and tools that are exclusive to the Maker, you can even cut wood with this machine. Balsa wood and basswood are two of the most common types of wood you can use in your Maker, up to 3/32″ thick. Like the Explore machines, the Maker machines have a dual tool holder, which means your machine can hold a blade and a pen at the same time. The Maker 3 is capable of cutting Smart Vinyl without a mat for cuts/designs larger than 11.5″ × 23.5″, which is the maximum cut size of the original Maker machine.

HEAT PRESSES

Let's chat about heat presses. A heat press is a machine that uses heat and pressure to bond materials. Heat presses are commonly used with iron-on material and garment customization, but can be used for so much more. You can even use a heat press on canvas, socks, shoes, wood, and the list goes on. I use two different presses in the projects that follow: a handheld EasyPress Mini and a 9″ × 9″ EasyPress 2. These aren't the only options for presses though. We'll start small.

HANDHELD PRESSES The EasyPress Mini or mini-iron is exactly what you need for those tiny personalized projects. The small size of these presses helps to monitor and manage the amount of heat you are applying to delicate projects.

SPECIALTY PRESSES Hats, mugs, and tumblers, oh my! Some full-size heat presses come with attachments that can be used to create a variety of projects. If you have a particular passion, it may be a wise investment to focus on one specific type of press. Cricut has a mug and a hat press, both of which are fun and user friendly.

EASYPRESS COLLECTION These come in a variety of sizes and colors. These handheld presses are a great option if you prefer a more portable heat press. They are available in 9″ × 9″ and 12″ × 10″ sizes. (Note that the 6″ × 7″ EasyPress is no longer available.) The 9″ × 9″ EasyPress is great for tote bags and other medium-sized projects, while the 12″ × 10″ is perfect for larger designs on shirts or canvases.

FULL-SIZE HEAT PRESS This is the way to go when you need more pressure or a larger heat plate. There are many options available across the Internet and in craft stores. Cricut also offers the Autopress machine, which is aimed toward professionals who produce batches of shirts or other goods. Full-size heat presses provide a great amount of space to make adult shirts and other items that need to be mass produced.

The above covers some essential points about each of the Cricut machines and tools. For more detailed information, check out *help.cricut.com*.

YOU'VE GOT YOUR CRICUT, NOW WHAT?

The first thing you'll want to do is get that beauty out of the box. Next, go to *design.cricut.com* or the App Store on your handheld device and download Cricut Design Space to install the necessary software. At first glance, Design Space can be confusing as there are so many tools, features, and options. I will introduce you to each of these functions in the pages and projects ahead to build your confidence to create any vision you may have.

I'll share images from Design Space from my computer, and please know the functions are the same whether you are using a tablet, phone, or other device.

When you sign into Design Space, you'll want to set up your machine. If you are not immediately prompted to do so when signing in, start by clicking on the three small horizontal lines in the upper-left corner to open the main menu, which looks like the image below. This is the menu to go to when you hit a snag. If you want to make stickers, I suggest starting with Calibration. This will ensure your Print Then Cut settings are precise (you may need to repeat this process every so often).

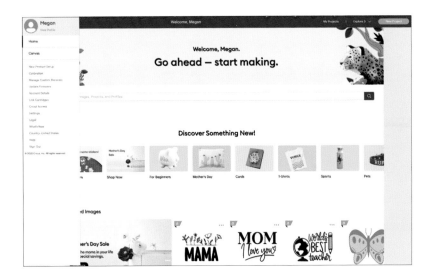

This is a great place to dig deeper into what your Cricut can do. Check out the Manage Custom Materials and you will discover all the different materials your machine can cut. Cricut Access is a subscription-based plan that gives you discounts on Cricut products as well as access to fonts, images, and features throughout Design Space. Cricut has a number of free images, shapes, and fonts, and their free offerings change regularly. The images used in this book are available through Cricut Access and many are also free.

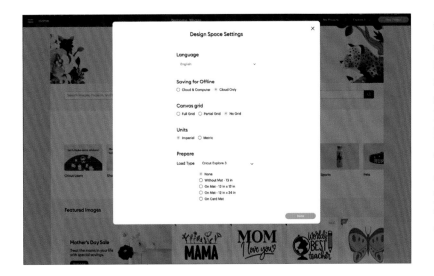

Within the Settings option you can choose how you want to set up your Design Space save options, grids, mat selection, and more. You can personalize Design Space to what works best with your design flow.

The large workspace in the center of your screen is called your canvas. This is where you will design and create, this is where the magic happens.

Now, let's take a tour down the options in the left column. Templates are fun to use to help you size a project or play around with simple mock-up designs. Take note that Templates are not available in the Design Space app on handheld devices.

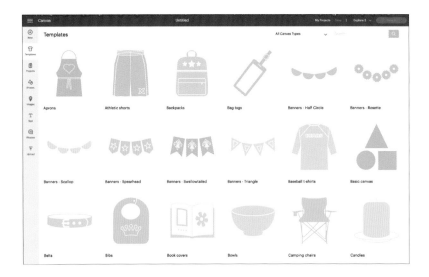

Projects are where you'll find Ready to Make projects that can be searched by category. Cricut has many projects available, including free projects, community projects, and featured projects, which can all be accessed through the Projects tab.

The Shapes tab is where you'll find a variety of basic shapes to add to your canvas. In the projects to follow we will reference these shapes often.

The Images tab is where you'll find access to over 250,000 images within the Design Space database. The search function allows you to find ready-to-use images for nearly any project you may be working on. There are also categories to access free, popular, recently added and featured images here. This is where you'll go to search for the images listed within the projects of this book. When searching for a specific image, you'll need to include the number symbol (#) followed by the letters and numbers.

The Text tab is where you'll go to add text to your canvas. This will bring up a text box and from there you can use the font drop down menu that comes up right above the canvas. With these options you can customize your text to the size, shape and specifications needed for your project. We'll dig into a few projects that use text within this book to get you more familiar with this feature.

The Phrases tab is much like the Images tab, but specifically for phrases. You can use the search function to see if Cricut has a phrase that fits your project needs.

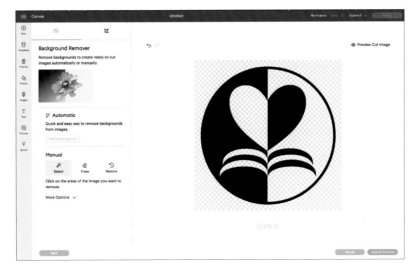

You'll want to get comfortable with the Upload function, especially if you like to create your own designs that you'll cut with your Cricut machine. You can also upload your own Pattern Fills in this tab. This tool is used in the Stickers for Goodie Bags project, found in the Let's Party chapter. When uploading your image or pattern fill, follow the prompts and make sure you upload a compatible format. If your image has a transparent background PNG or a SVG file, you can upload it without any modifications. If your image has a simple background, you can easily remove the background with the Background Remover tool, or manually select each section you'd like to remove with the wand tool. Then save your image as a Cut image or a Print Then Cut image. See the images here for before and after references of removing the white parts of the design with the wand tool.

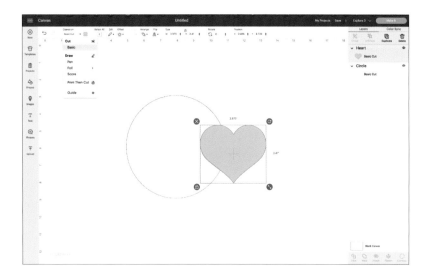

Now let's go over the tools you'll find across the top menu of your canvas, the Edit Bar. To the far left, you'll see there is an undo and redo button. Next is a drop-down menu labeled Operation. These tools are fun to play with when creating your own designs. We'll use quite a few of these functions in the projects in this book to get you more familiar with what each of them can do. If you'll be using the Print Then Cut operation, take note that the maximum printing space (at the time of writing) is 6.75″ × 9.25″.

PRO TIP

If you want to make a full sheet of stickers, or another print-able project, start with a 6.75″ × 9.25″ rectangle and then continue to design your project inside the rectangle. Another tip is to change the operation of this rectangle layer from a Basic Cut to Guide. The Guide layer will not be seen on the Make It screen; it will simply be used as a template while creating the design on the canvas.

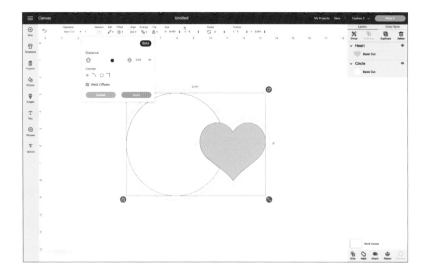

In the next section you'll find Select All, Edit and the Off-set tool. Offset is a tool that Cricut crafters waited years to see show up in Design Space! It was worth the wait, and I use it in many of my projects. It makes creating layers for shaker cards, cake toppers, and stickers so much easier than using another program and uploading each element. The Offset tool works with a single layer or multiple layers. It creates an additional layer that can be used as a back-ground or shadow layer.

Next, you'll see Align, Arrange, and Flip. These functions are used to adjust your images. Use Align when you have more than one layer selected and you need to align them to one another. This is also where you'll find the ability to evenly distribute the spacing between several selected layers/images.

The Arrange function is used when you want to move the layers forward or backward on your canvas. Arrange is used several times throughout the projects in this book, giving you a chance to see first-hand when and how to use this function.

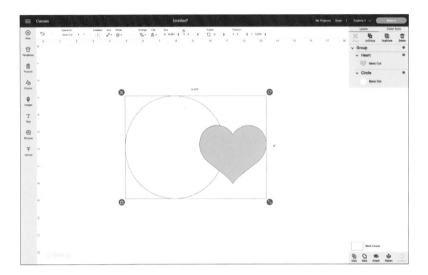

Let's move over to the panel on the far right of the screen, which is where you'll find your Layers and Color Sync tools. In the Layers panel, the Group function allows you to select multiple layers and resize or move them as one layer. In the image here you can see that I have grouped the two shapes on my canvas. While they will move on the canvas as one, when you get to the Make It screen, they will not cut as shown.

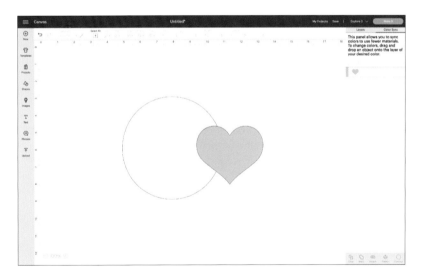

The Color Sync tool is great to use when working with multiple layers of different colors. It can help to organize your cuts and make the cutting process easier. When you tap into the Color Sync tool, you'll see this prompt, "This panel allows you to sync colors to use fewer materials. To change colors, drag and drop an object onto the layer of your desired color."

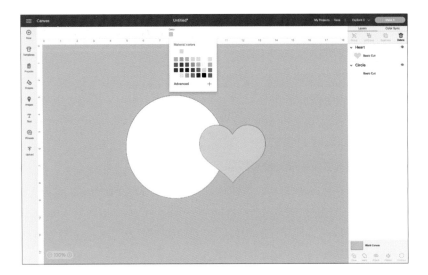

Speaking of color, see that little white box labeled Blank Canvas near the bottom of the Layers panel? If you click on that white box, you can change the color of your canvas. This is helpful if you're trying to visualize what a project will look like with a specific background color. You can choose from any of the colors shown or tap the + icon and pick any custom color you need. This option is also helpful if you're working with sticker sheets that are white and you want to see the edges of your design more clearly.

Back to the Layers panel, let's go through the functions on the bottom row. Each of these tools and functions can be used in a variety of ways so my suggestion is to bring some shapes onto your canvas and play around with them. Keep in mind that what you see on your canvas might not be what you see on the Make It screen, unless you use the proper functions. Let's dig into what each of these functions can do.

The Slice tool takes two overlapping layers and creates cut paths where they intersect. This creates new layers, as shown in the images below. In the first image you can see that new layers have been created in the Layers panel. For the second image I've separated the shapes like puzzle pieces so you can see how it all fits together.

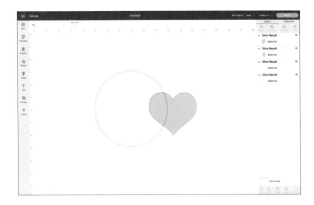
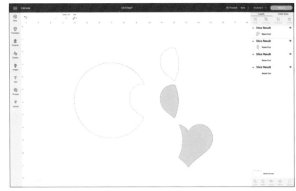

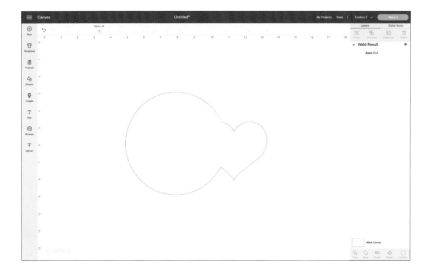

The Weld tool is used when you want to convert many layers into a single new cut path. Also note, because you are transforming several layers into one new cut path, they will become the same color. The image here shows how the circle and heart have been welded together to create one shape. Sometimes it's helpful to use this tool toward the end of your project when everything is just how you want it on your canvas. Keep in mind there is no unweld function, but if need be you can use the undo button. Once you save your project you cannot undo a Weld. I suggest using this function when working with script/connected text so your text flows as if it was handwritten smoothly.

The Attach tool is used when you want to keep your images, text, and operations as they are on the canvas when you Make It. We'll use this several times throughout the projects in this book, which will help you to further understand the many ways this tool can be used. In the images below you can see that on the canvas both layers are selected and Attached. Then in the next image you can see that they appear on the Make It screen in the exact layout. This tool is also needed when working with text layers (not script, see Weld). In order to get your text to be cut exactly as you see it on your canvas, you'll want to select the text layer and then Attach. Also note that when layers are Attached, the button changes to a Detach tool, this can be used any time throughout the design process to separate any attached layers.

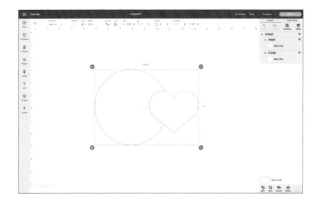
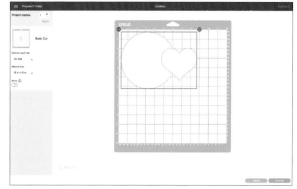

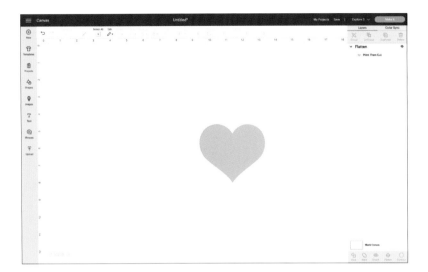

The Flatten tool will be used when you want to Print Then Cut your project. In the image here you can see that the two shapes layers have now been turned into one Print Then Cut layer. Your Cricut will only cut around the outside of your flattened layer. If you're creating stickers, this will be a well-used tool.

The Contour tool is a fun tool with many uses. This tool can be used to eliminate small details within your image or to remove any cuts within your image that you don't want in your final project. Here is a sample project of how we can change this MOM image into a version with the heart inside the O.

Start out by searching for this MOM image #M37DAC from the Images tab and this heart shape which can be found in the Shapes tab. The end goal is to eliminate the circle in the letter O and replace it with the heart shape.

Click the Contour tool and a pop-up window will show you all the different cut lines in the right column. You can either hover your mouse and click on the section you'd like to remove (it will switch from light gray to dark gray when selected), or you can use the column on the right side to select which layers you'd like to remove.

Exit out of that pop-up window and you'll see that your image has changed on the canvas. It should look like the image here.

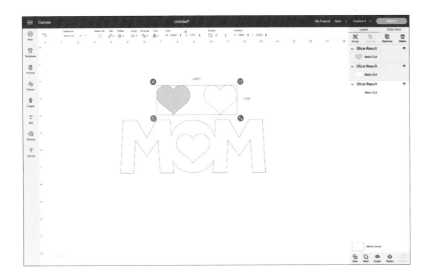

Now you can click and drag the heart to move it into the middle of the O and then select both layers. Next, use the Slice tool. Once sliced you can see in the image here that the heart shape has been cut from the MOM image. The hearts have been moved above the image to show the different layers that have been created.

Now delete the two isolated hearts and you're left with a new MOM image with a heart in the center. Super cute!

If your Design Space doesn't look exactly like the images shown throughout this book, please know that Cricut updates their apps regularly; however, the tools and functions are still the same, even if the images look different. Also, the steps and design processes in this book are just one way of creating these projects. The fun thing about crafting with Cricut is there are several ways to achieve the same results. Have fun and find what works for you!

TOOLS & ACCESSORIES

There are a few tools you'll need before you can get started crafting with your Cricut, let's go over some must have items and useful tools of the trade.

Let's go over hand tools first. In the image on the next page you'll see a variety of tools that will be used in this book.

BRAYER This roller is one of my favorite hand tools. This tool was created to apply fabric smoothly to the Cricut mat; however, I've found that I use this on nearly all my materials when applying them to the Cricut mat. The brayer rolls out any air bubbles and ensures that your material is securely in place on your mat.

SCRAPER TOOLS These tools are not only great for applying your vinyl and transfer tapes, but also for cleaning your mats when there is paper left behind. Simply scrape all those scraps away and right into the trash. You can also use a handheld squeegee or a credit card as a substitute for a scraper tool.

WEEDING TOOLS You'll need some sort of sharp weeding tool when working with vinyl or iron-on material. These tools are used to pick up and "weed out" any of the material that is not part of your final design. I've shown a few examples in the image and there are many more; as long as it is comfortable for you to use, and it works—use it.

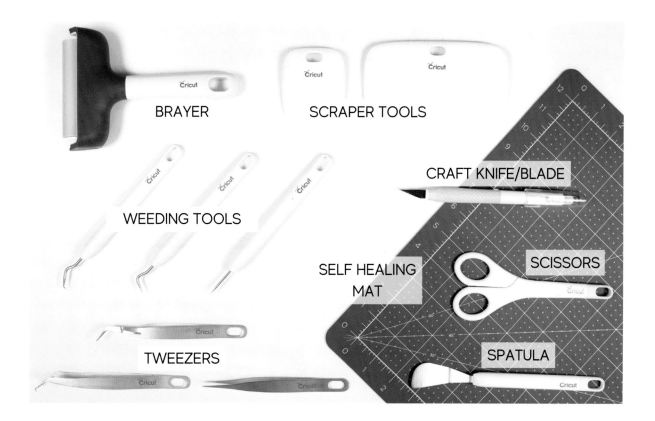

BRAYER

SCRAPER TOOLS

WEEDING TOOLS

CRAFT KNIFE/BLADE

SELF HEALING MAT

SCISSORS

TWEEZERS

SPATULA

PRO TIP

If you have a favorite mechanical pencil with a squishy grip you can turn it into a weeding tool. Simply take out all the lead inside your pencil and drop a sewing needle into the barrel. It may take a moment to find the right size sewing needle, so start small and work your way up until you can retract the needle just like you would a standard piece of lead.

CRAFT KNIFE/BLADE This little blade comes in very handy whenever you need to cut something quickly. I recommend pairing it with a self-healing mat to make sure you're protecting your workspace.

SCISSORS These Cricut scissors come with a sheath, which is great, because these scissors are SHARP!

TWEEZERS There are several types of tweezers here. Your standard tweezers with both a pointed and an angled tip, as well as a pair of reverse tweezers. Reverse tweezers are great for paper crafts; you can pick up the paper with the tweezers and hold them in place until you squeeze the tweezers to let them go.

SPATULA This is just like the spatula you'd find in your kitchen, but it's smaller, cuter, and made for crafting. With the spatula you can easily remove your paper projects from the Cricut mat to prevent your paper from curling.

CRICUT MACHINE MATS

You'll also need a mat to place your material on when using your Cricut unless you're using the Cricut Explore Air 3 or Maker 3 machines, which have the capability of matless cutting. Cricut machine mats are available in a variety of colors and sizes, and each color has specific materials it is designed to work best with.

> **PRO TIP**
>
> When cutting matless with your Air 3 or Maker 3 machines you may want to invest in a Cricut Roll Holder; this handy device keeps your bulk rolls tidy while cutting and also comes with a built-in trimmer tool to cut off your material when the cuts are complete.

Let's get into specifics about which mat to use and when. Remember to save the clear liners that come with your mats and reapply them after each project. This will keep them cleaner, which could extend the life of your mats.

BLUE LightGrip Machine Mat is used when cutting lightweight materials like light cardstock, copy paper, vellum, and other materials that might rip easily with a stronger grip mat.

GREEN StandardGrip Machine Mat is for medium-weight materials like vinyl, iron-on material, and heavier cardstock.

PURPLE StrongGrip Machine Mat is suggested for heavy-duty materials like cardboard, thick cardstock, glitter cardstock, wood, poster board, and magnet material.

PINK FabricGrip Machine Mat was created specifically for cutting fabrics with your Cricut machine.

When your mats start to lose their stickiness or become dirty, you can easily wash your mats and they will be almost as good as new. My favorite way to renew/clean my mats is to put them under running water and use a bristled scrub brush with a little bit of dish soap and scrub lightly all over the mat. When the debris has been gently scrubbed away, you can rinse your mat and hang to dry. Once the mat is dry, simply put the clear liner back on top of it and store it away for the next time you get crafty.

CRICUT BLADES

Depending on your machine and craft project, the instructions may call for a specific blade. Your new machine will always come with a Fine-Point Blade, which is called for in almost all the projects in this book. Each machine has a different housing (where you put the blades into the machine) and not all blades work with each machine.

The Cricut Joy has one slot, which can be used for the Fine-Point Blade it comes with, a pen/marker, or the Joy Foil Transfer Tool.

The Cricut Explore series has two slots in the carriage, labeled side A (left) and B (right). In the left side (A), you can use a Scoring Stylus/Tool or a pen/marker. On the right side (B), you can use the Fine-Point Blade or one of the other specialty blades made for this machine, as mentioned below.

DEEP-POINT BLADE This blade and housing is black. This blade is great for using with thicker materials like foam, cardboard, chipboard, and stiffened felt.

BONDED-FABRIC BLADE This blade and housing is pink and matches the FabricGrip mat. The Explore series can cut fabric, but it needs to be bonded or have an iron-on backer.

FOIL TRANSFER TOOL This tool is blue. This tool is used several times throughout this book to add foil detailing to both leather and cardstock. This tool comes with three tips: fine, medium, and bold.

The Maker machines are where Cricut really stepped up the blades and tools. Not only can you use all the tools that you can use with the Explore machines, but there's something special about the carriage on the Maker machines. There is a gear hiding behind that Fine-Point Blade. This is used when working with the blades listed below.

ROTARY BLADE This little blade really packs a punch! Not only can you use it for delicate materials like tissue paper, but you can also use it for cutting thicker materials like denim and other fabrics. Cricut recommends keeping your images larger than 3/4″ when using the Rotary Blade, as smaller images may damage your mat and/or blade.

KNIFE BLADE This tool is a game changer! This is the blade that allows your Cricut Maker to cut basswood, balsa wood, and other materials up to 3/32″ (2.4mm) thick. Reminder: When cutting thicker materials, make sure to move the white star wheels on the silver roller bar to the side so you don't leave imprints on your material.

The following tools are called QuickSwap Tools. They are only made for the Maker machines and can all be swapped out using the same housing.

SCORING WHEEL & DOUBLE SCORING WHEEL These tools provide 10x more pressure than the Scoring Stylus/Tool used in the Explore series. Creating score lines for cards and treat boxes has never been easier. Use the Double Scoring Wheel when scoring thicker materials like cardboard.

DEBOSSING TIP This tool creates depressions (indents) into a variety of impressionable materials. You can transform plain material into a patterned and textured creation to be used in your next craft, or as a standalone decoration in your home or office.

ENGRAVING TIP This tip can create engraved designs on metal, glass, leather, acrylic, and more!

PERFORATION BLADE This blade cuts perforated lines that can be used to create coupon books, raffle tickets, unique cards, and more! Making a peek-a-boo card with a tearable element is a great way to use this blade.

WAVY BLADE This blade creates a fun, wavy edge along your fancy or playful creations. You can create unique envelopes, cards, badges, gift tags… anything that you'd want to add a special edge to!

Now that you've got the rundown of Design Space, tools, and accessories, let's start making!

happy
everything

be
JOYFUL

CHAPTER ONE

Home Decor and More

Having a Cricut means you can label and customize ALL THE THINGS! Signs, drinkware, journals...these are just the tip of the iceberg! You can customize these projects to fit your personal style and aesthetic to craft a cozy home for yourself, your friends and family, or start a business!

Bookmark with Foil

Creating custom bookmarks with your Cricut is a breeze! Grab some faux or genuine leather and find your favorite witty book-related pun and you're all set. For this bookmark we'll be using Cricut's Foil Transfer tool to create a sophisticated keepsake.

Materials Needed

- Faux or genuine leather
- Foil Transfer tool
- Foil Transfer sheets
- Washi or painter's tape
- Craft knife (optional)
- Ruler (optional)
- Self-healing mat (optional)
- Glue gun or leather adhesive

Machine Compatibility

Any Cricut machine

Images Used

Stack of Books #M231CE56F
Rectangle #M7F037EA
Oval #M2AAB3D97

DESIGN IT

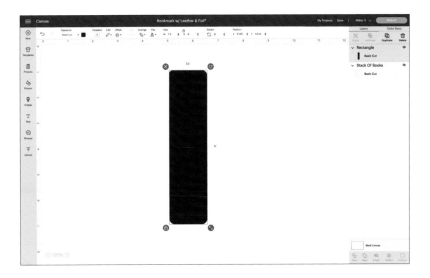

Start with your overall desired shape. If you choose a rectangle, decide whether you want rounded or squared corners. Add the shape to your Design Space canvas and size it to your liking. I went with a rectangle with rounded corners and sized it 1.5″ × 6″.

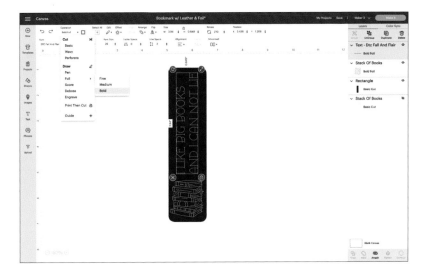

Now comes the fun part of adding your text and any images you like by using the Text tab on the left side of your canvas. Adjust the sizes and alignment of your design elements at this time. In the image here, you can see in the Layers panel that the Basic Cut layer of the book image is hidden. You can hide layers by tapping the eye/hide icon. In the Operation dropdown menu, change the text and image by selecting Foil, then Bold.

PRO TIP
Use a font that is labeled as a Writing font. This will give the best results for creating your foil text.

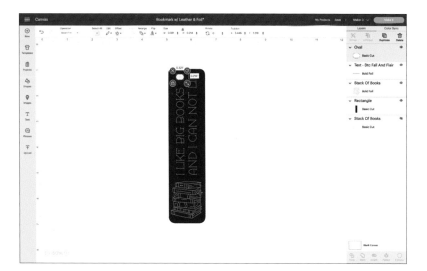

What's a bookmark without a tassel? Okay, it can still be a bookmark, just a little less fun. If you'd like your bookmark to have a tassel, add a shape to serve as the hole to attach your tassel. I chose an oval because I'll make my tassel out of leather scraps and need a little more width. More on that in a minute.

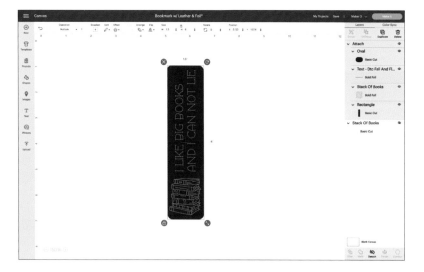

When your design is the way you want it, in the Layers panel, click on all the layers and then click on Attach, as shown here. (You can delete the Basic Cut layer that will be hidden, but you don't have to.)

MAKE IT

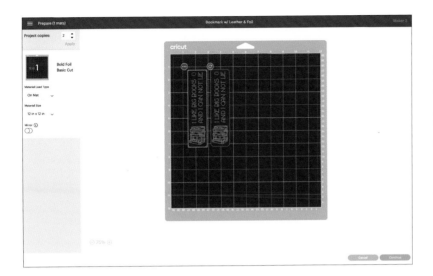

Now you're ready to click on the green Make It button. Once on the Make It screen, move your project down into the grid a bit. I brought mine down just a bit more than 1″ from the top and 1″ from the left side. Keep this positioning in mind as you place your leather onto your mat. The reason for doing this is to give some clearance around your material so it doesn't hit the star wheels (small white wheels) on the bar of your machine or leave imprints on your material.

The Foil Transfer tool process is a bit different than just cutting your material straightaway. You'll need to start by laying the foil over your leather material, keeping in mind where your leather and the designs are on the Make It screen. Using the tape that comes with the foil transfer sheets, or washi or painter's tape, make sure you tape all four edges of the foil down. Try to make the foil as smooth and secure as you can—if it's not taped well, your foil will shift.

Before you start your machine, swap out your Fine-Point Blade for the Bold Foil Transfer tip (the one with three lines), then follow the prompts on your screen. When this first process is complete, remove the foil but do not unload your mat. Just slide the foil out from underneath the carriage. Next, swap out the Foil Transfer tool for your Fine-Point Blade and then cut the material.

When the cutting process is complete, you can begin to assemble your bookmark. All it needs now is a tassel. You can make a tassel out of yarn, ribbon, or even the leather scraps from this project. If you'd like to create your tassel out of leather scraps, read on for a few suggestions.

MAKE IT **EXTRA**

Faux leather is perfect for a bookmark because it is thin enough that it won't cause your book to warp or bulge, but it is sturdy enough to use book after book. Have fun with the types of leathers, designs, and text to customize bookmarks for all the book-loving people in your life!

Using the leather scraps as the tassel also makes this bookmark a bit extra. You'll need a ruler, craft blade, and a self-healing mat. You can use scissors for the next step, but it might become a bit tedious. Using the excess leather (scraps from your project), create a small, thin rectangle to use as your tassel. See the image above for an example of what your leather scraps may look like and what section may be useful to use as your tassel.

From there you can make a small slit about 1/3″ in from one end. This will be used to create a lark's head knot. I took this a step further and split the rest of the leather in thirds lengthwise to create a bit of a fringe. Just be sure to leave some room between the initial slice and your new fringe. Then loop it through the hole in the bookmark.

Secure the end of the leather to the back of the bookmark as shown here. You're all set with a unique and personalized bookmark!

happy everything

Felt Banner

Felt banners are so versatile! The soft texture of the felt, along with the beauty of the iron-on, can add a homey touch to any room. For this project you can use either the Maker or Explore machine and the outcome will be the same, but the process is different. The Maker uses a Rotary Blade to cut the felt easily, while the Explore requires any fabric to be bonded. However, you can easily cut the felt banner by hand no matter what machine you choose to use.

Materials

Felt
Iron-on material
Weeding tool
Heat press
Heat press mat
Felt glue/adhesive
Wooden dowel
Ribbon/jute

If using a Maker:
Rotary Blade

If using an Explore:
Tools to cut banner (scissors, craft blade, rotary cutter, ruler, self-healing mat)

Machine Compatibility

Maker or Explore series (and cut the banner by hand)

Images Used

Rectangle #M2AAB3E02
Flowers #M33FB83A6

Flowers #M338F1DBC
Pennant #M2AAB3EE0

DESIGN IT

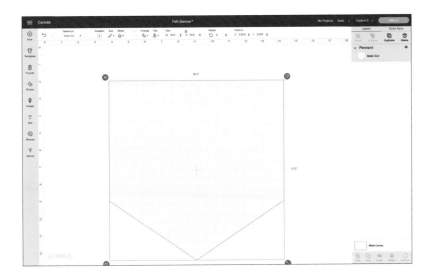

I'll be designing the whole project in Design Space and depending on which machine you're using, you can either cut the felt with the Maker or Rotary Blade. If you're using an Explore machine, you can cut the felt by hand, as mentioned on the previous page.

Begin by bringing the Pennant image (#M2AAB3EE0) onto your canvas. I've sized mine to 10.5″ × 10.5″, as shown here. Your final size will depend on the size of your felt, so be sure to measure your felt first.

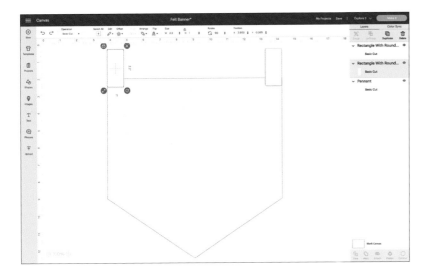

Tabs will be used to hang the banner on a wooden dowel, so add two small rectangles to your canvas as well. I used the Rounded Rectangles (#M2AAB3E02) and then aligned them to the upper-left and upper-right corners of the banner, as shown here. Size each tab 1″ wide and a little more than 2″ long. Position the tabs so they overlap the banner image just a bit.

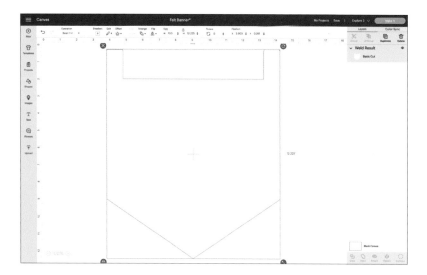

Next, select all three layers and then click on Weld. This will create one cut around the perimeter of the three layers combined. Next, you can decorate the banner with any text or images you like.

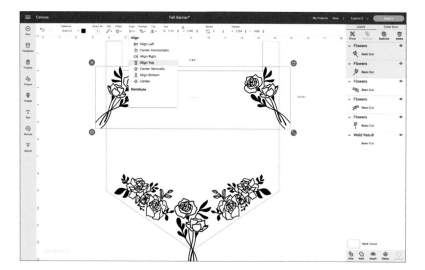

The flowers shown here make a beautiful addition to this banner. If you want your banner to be (mostly) symmetrical, just bring one of each flower onto your canvas, then you can use the tools found on the Edit Bar to duplicate, flip, resize, and otherwise edit the designs to fit your banner. In the image here you can see I used the two flower images, but I duplicated, rotated, and flipped them to create a symmetrical border on the banner. I suggest using the Align tool to make sure everything is centered and matching.

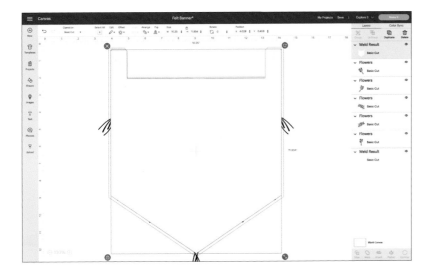

You may have noticed the flowers are hanging off the edges of this banner. Let's take care of that. This next step is optional but might give you a cleaner-looking result than if you trimmed them by hand. Start by duplicating the background banner layer and shrinking it a bit, creating an even border all the way around the outer edges, like the image here (see the stems hanging over the edges).

You can only Slice two layers at a time, so select the small banner layer and one flower, and work your way around to each of the three flowers and then Slice. This will create extra layers, but go ahead and delete those as you go. Keep only your banner and freshly trimmed flowers. You should end up with something similar to the image here.

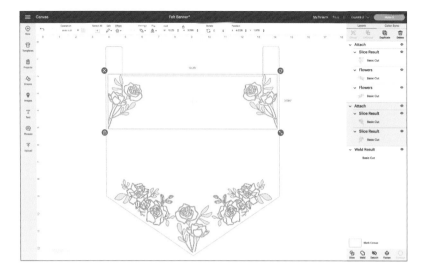

To make the cutting and assembly part easy and precise, I suggest selecting the top two flower layers and then click on Attach; this will keep your images in place and aligned when it comes time for your machine to cut. Repeat this process for the bottom three flowers, like the image here shows. Changing the colors of the layers can also be done at this time, so when you add your text in the next step, your machine will know that you want multiple materials/colors to be used.

Now you can add any text you like on your canvas. I added "happy everything" and used the Weld function for each line of text. I also clicked on Attach for the two lines of text so it will cut exactly as shown on the canvas. This eliminates possible mishaps with mis-alignment when it comes time to heat press your project.

PRO TIP

If you're working with a script/cursive font, I suggest using the Weld option so the text will be cut in one smooth path. If you select Attach instead of Weld, the cuts between the letters will still be there.

MAKE IT

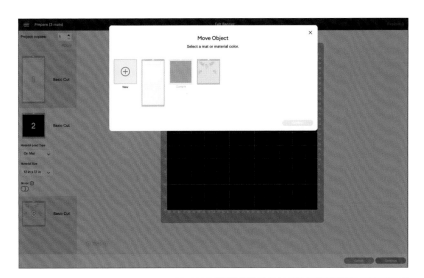

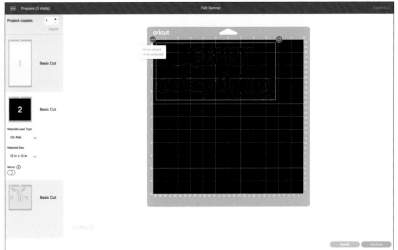

Now you're ready to click on the green Make It button. Here are a few tips to save time and material, and to make the heat pressing part a bit easier. On the Make It screen, you can arrange your elements on one mat (if they fit). Do this by selecting the image you'd like to move to another mat and click on the three dots in the upper-left corner of the image, then select Move Object. When prompted, select the mat you'd like to move the image to; in this case it's mat 3 (as shown here). Remember to adjust the Mirror settings and make sure to toggle ON for the mats that you'll be using iron-on with. As a general rule, basic iron-on is placed shiny side down on the cutting mat and mirrored. This is so when you flip it over to heat press, your text/images will be correct.

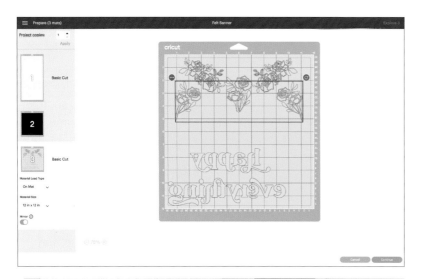

To take this a step further and save a bit of material, you can move the flowers up closer together. This helps maintain their alignment after everything is cut. The image here shows how the final mat looks on the Make It screen, and also how you should set up the mat with iron-on to be cut, if you've chosen to move all of your iron-on material onto one mat.

PRO TIP

Using a brayer on all the materials will help them adhere to the mat during the cutting process.

When cutting your felt, make sure to swap out the Fine-Point Blade for the Rotary Blade as shown here.

Check that your machine has cut all the way through the felt before unloading your mat.

PRO TIP
It's a good idea to peel back a corner of your material BEFORE unloading your mat. If your material doesn't cut through on the initial cut, press the cut button again.

When you insert your iron-on material mat into the machine put the Fine-Point Blade back in.

Now that all your materials have been cut, grab your weeding tool and remove all the unnecessary pieces of your iron-on, leaving only your design.

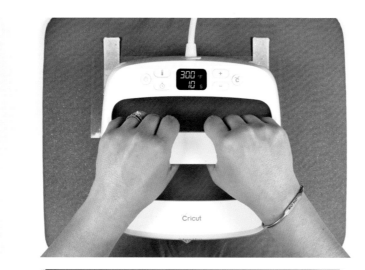

On your heat press mat, lay down your felt with the iron-on design positioned where you want it, then follow the instructions for your particular iron-on material and apply the heat press for the designated time and temperature settings. Also note if your iron-on material requires a warm or cool/cold peel. Specialty materials often call for a cool/cold peel to allow the material to bond before removing the carrier sheet. As instructed by your material specifications, remove the clear carrier sheet slowly, making sure your iron-on material has adhered well to the felt. If your iron-on material looks like it's not adhered well, apply the heat press with more pressure for just a few more seconds.

Now is the time to add the wooden dowel. Flip your banner over and glue the ends of the tabs down, leaving enough room to feed the wooden dowel through, as shown here.

Finally, attach your favorite ribbon, string, yarn, or jute on either side of the wooden dowel, leaving enough slack to hang your new banner.

MAKE IT **EXTRA**

There's so much more you can do with this project idea! Once your felt banner is complete you can add tassels, ribbon curls, or pom-poms to each end of the wooden dowel. These cute banners would make the sweetest birth announcements in a nursery, or a fun learning tool in a classroom or playroom. With any text or designs, you can transform this idea to fit any style or theme!

Glass Etching

Etching glass can turn a basic champagne flute, wine glass, canning jar, casserole dish, or cutting board into a custom piece of professional-looking art. Etched champagne flutes make great gifts for newlyweds too, so let's make a matching set!

Materials Needed

Glass surface (champagne flutes)
Stencil film/removable vinyl
Transfer tape/paper
Weeding tool
Scraper tool
Etching cream
Protective gloves and eyewear
Paint or foam brush
Running water or basin for rinsing

Machine Compatibility

Any Cricut machine

DESIGN IT

Begin by measuring your blank glass surface. How much room do you have to work with? For these champagne flutes the maximum width, I'd suggest is 2.25″. This measurement will make the text large enough to be transferred nicely and will be legible without wrapping too far around the glass. You can use any text or image you like, but try to keep your designs on the simple side until you've tested your materials and have become familiar with the process.

Make sure you Weld the layers of each surface you'll be etching. For example, in the image below, you can see that "Mr." and "Mrs." have been welded on two separate layers. This will allow for you to move these layers independently on the Make It screen, which is important.

Also, because a script font was used here, welding creates a single cut path around the letters, as if you were writing Mr. and Mrs. in cursive. When your design is ready, click the green Make It button.

MAKE IT

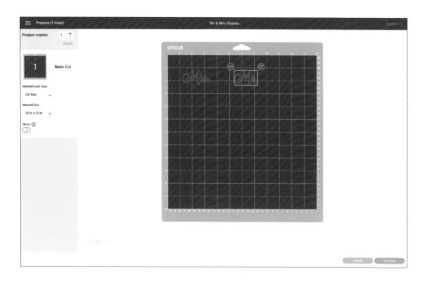

On the Make It screen, move your designs over and down a bit by clicking and dragging each design. This will allow enough room to cut around your stencil and will also provide a border around your design so you can apply the etching cream without getting any unwanted cream on your surface.

Cut your designs and then weed the design from your stencil material. Typically, for a vinyl decal, you'd remove the negative space; however, for stencils the process is reversed (in this case you remove the letters).

After your design has been fully weeded, apply a piece of transfer tape over your design. You can see in the image here my transfer tape doesn't fully cover the stencil material, which is OK. You want the transfer tape to just cover your image so you can transfer all those fine details. Make sure to use a scraper tool to get good adhesion between the transfer tape and your stencil material and also to remove any possible air bubbles.

Gently peel the stencil material off its backing, making sure to pick up any small pieces of vinyl that may be left behind. Then apply your stencil material to your glass surface, again using your scraper tool to remove any possible air bubbles. If there are bubbles and gaps, the etching cream might leak into those spots and etch unwanted parts of your glass.

When you're sure you've got a good seal around your design, gently peel away the transfer tape. You'll see in the image here there are creases in the stencil material, but the design itself has a great seal all the way around it. When you wrap flat material on a curved surface there are bound to be wrinkles and creases, and that's OK. Just make sure that your design is adhered well. You can even go back over the stencil with your scraper tool or fingers to make sure it's on there securely.

Always wear protective gloves and eyewear when working with etching cream. Using your paint or foam brush, apply the etching cream over your stencil. Gentle tapping and dabbing motions will work best to apply the etching cream. Once the cream has been spread over your entire design, you can swirl the cream around to make sure you've got full coverage.

Refer to the directions on your particular etching cream to see how long you should leave the solution on your surface. When the time is up, rinse off your glass with the stencil still on it, making sure you wash off all the etching cream. Dry your surface and then slowly peel away the stencil material. Wash your surface again just to be sure there isn't any etching cream on your glass after removing the stencil.

NOTE

When your surface is still wet it might look like the etching didn't work, but as it dries you will see the magic appear!

MAKE IT **EXTRA**

Have fun playing with different images and text! For these glasses you could apply the couple's names on the other side of the glass, or perhaps the anniversary date. If you're customizing a mirror, a plaque, or some other glass surface that won't be washed regularly, you can use a pigmented metallic finish like Rub 'n Buff to create a lustrous look on your newly etched surface. This really brings out the detail, but you would lose the frosty look of the etching. And remember that a little Rub 'n Buff goes a long way.

Custom Labels

One of the perks of owning a Cricut machine is the ability to label all the things! You can use this project idea to create labels for your pantry, closet, office, or craft room! Smart Paper Sticker Cardstock is really the hero here. You can also use Smart Label Writable Paper if you're using a Cricut Joy.

Materials Needed

Sticker cardstock
Cricut pen

Machine Compatibility

Any Cricut machine

Images Used

Weapons of Mass Creation #M284FDE7E
Art Utensils Bag Design #M284FE001
Rounded Corner Label #M10E79A3D

DESIGN IT

Although you can make labels for anything in your house, let's start with a project for your craft space. This Weapons of Mass Creation image is cute as is, but I decided to edit the crayons out and add the variety of the Art Utensils image. This project will show several techniques within Design Space to edit an image.

Start by bringing the images listed on the previous page onto your canvas.

Next, Detach the Weapons of Mass Creation image and delete everything except the text and lines layers. You should be left with four layers, like the image here.

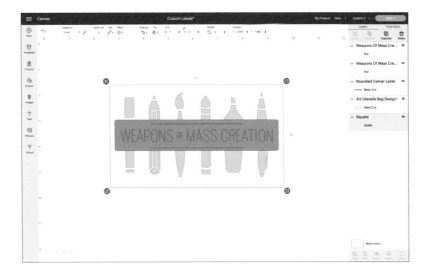

Before you go any further, measure the surface where you plan to put your label. The storage caddy used in this project has a maximum area of 7″ × 4″. Create a rectangle shape with those dimensions, and from the Edit Bar, set the Operation type to Guide for that layer. Guide layers do not cut on the final Make It screen, they only serve as a template while designing. Arrange the images within your Guide as shown here. This won't be the final design but is just a rough draft for sizing.

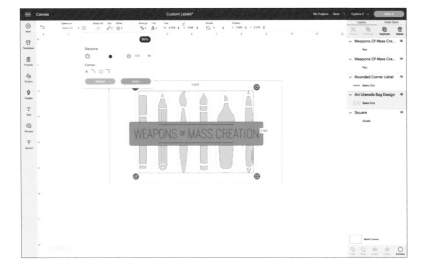

Play with stretching and resizing your images to your liking, and then from the Edit Bar select the Art Utensils layer and create a thin offset of about 0.15″.

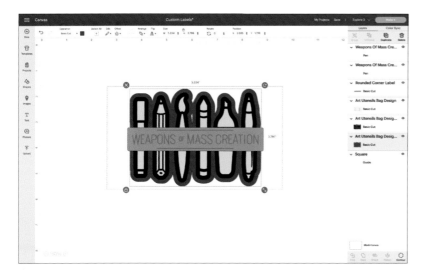

Next, select your new offset layer and do one more offset. You should have something that resembles the image here.

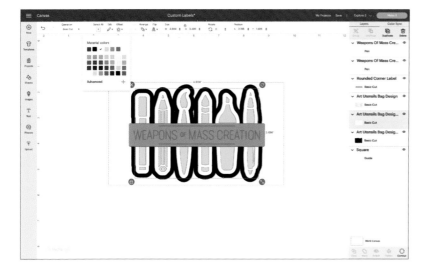

Now that all the elements are there, it's time to fine-tune the operations, colors, and final-cut appearance. Working from the outside in, let's change the colors of the offset layers by selecting the desired offset layer and then clicking the colored square next to the Operation menu at the top of your canvas.

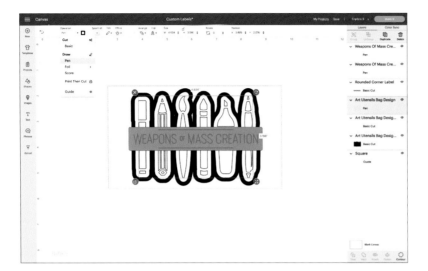

Next, change the Operation of the original Art Utensils layer from Basic Cut to Pen, and change the color of the pen by going back to the square next to the Operation menu and selecting your desired pen and color.

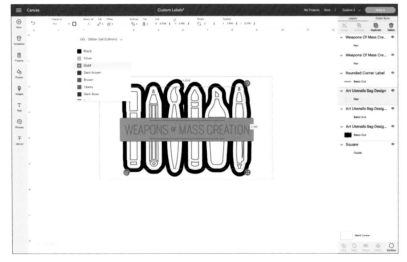

We're halfway there! Next up is to work on the Rounded Corner Label layer. Select that layer and change the color to match your sticker cardstock. Also change the color of your pen for the writing across the label.

Duplicate the Rounded Corner Label layer and arrange it directly behind the one that is currently there. You can do this by selecting the layer you'd like to move and clicking the Arrange function in the Edit Bar, then selecting Send Backward. The next step is to select the Art Utensils pen layer and one of the Rounded Corner Label layers, then Slice. You'll then remove three of the four new layers that the slicing tool just created, leaving only the Pen layer of the Art Utensils layer, as shown here.

Let's start combining some of these layers now. Select the first offset layer (white layer) and the Rounded Corner Label layer and Weld them to become a single layer. This new layer will move to the top of the stack, so you'll need to select that layer and Arrange it to Send Backward until all the pen layers show again. Next, select all the pen layers plus your new welded layer and Attach them. Your Cricut will now recognize that all those elements are on one layer. Although the images from the previous step and the one shown here look the same, look at the layers panel and you will see they are different. Also, check the Make It screen to make sure it looks like the image here. If not, go back through the steps and make sure to Attach the layers where needed.

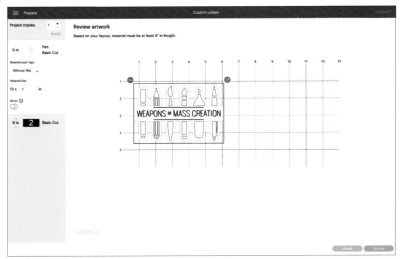

MAKE IT

After all those steps, the machine does most of the remaining work. Click on the green Make It button and load your sticker cardstock into your machine. Follow the prompts that will tell you which pen to put in first and when it's time to switch pens.

Look how cool this sticker cardstock is. Simply peel off the backing and lay the offset layer onto your surface. No transfer tape necessary!

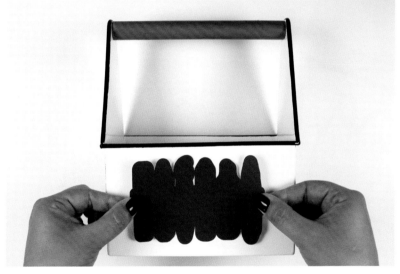

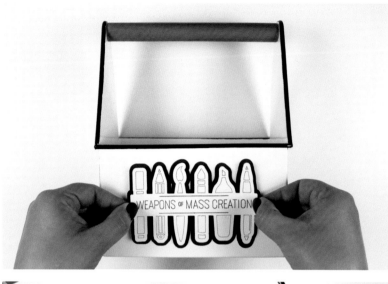

Next, peel the backing off your second layer, center it, and then apply it on top of the background layer. That's it!

MAKE IT **EXTRA**

These labels can be made large or small. You can design custom labels for jars, candles, drawers, storage pieces… literally, anything you can put a sticker on!

Reverse Canvas

Did you know that most art canvases are wrapped around the most beautiful wooden frames? Truly! For this project we will take one of those wrapped canvases and unwrap it, take it apart, and then put it back together again—but backwards. If this sounds confusing, don't worry, I'll break it down for you and you'll be a pro in no time!

Materials Needed

Iron-on material (also known as heat transfer vinyl)

Wrapped canvas (from craft or dollar store)

Craft knife

Weeding tool

Heat press

Heat press pad

Glue gun/strong adhesive

Machine Compatibility

Any Cricut machine (depending on size of canvas/design)

Image Used

Wash Your Hands #M14756BED

DESIGN IT

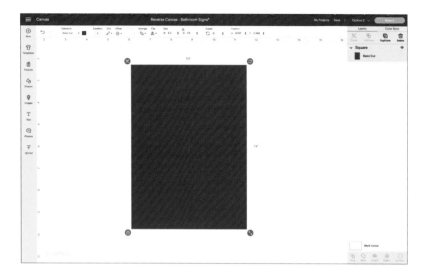

Before you start designing, measure the dimensions of the inside of the frame. The canvas frame used in this project is 8″ × 10″. To create a bit of a border around the image and the inside of the frame, begin with a rectangle that is 5.5″ × 7.5″ in Design Space.

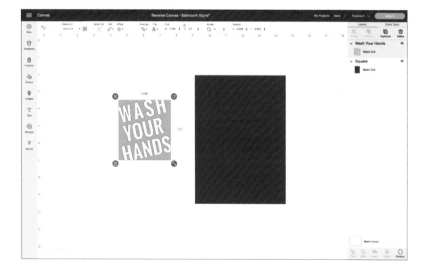

Next, insert whatever image you'd like to add to your sign. I'll be hanging this sign in the bathroom so my kiddos can have a gentle reminder to wash their hands.

When your design is ready to go, size it to fit inside the rectangle on your canvas. I like to leave a bit of a border between the frame and the design, as you can see here.

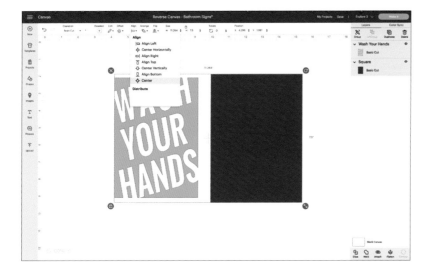

With the two layers selected, click on Align and then select Center in the drop-down, as shown here.

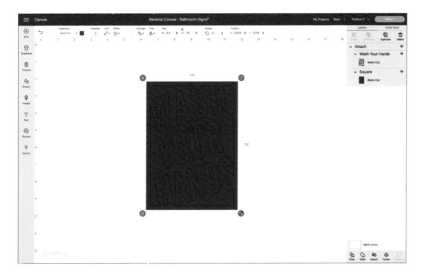

With everything centered, the next step is to Attach both layers. You can see here, this creates a border and also changes the color of the layers to be the same. Your Cricut will now cut these two layers just as they show on the Design Space screen, from one piece of material.

MAKE IT

Now click on the green Make It button. On the Make It screen, check that you toggle the Mirror option, especially if your image has text. Remember to place the iron-on material shiny side down on the mat.

As your machine is cutting, let's go ahead and remove the canvas from the frame. Grab a craft knife/blade and carefully cut around the back of the canvas, as shown here.

After cutting all around the frame, remove any leftover strips of canvas. You can remove the staples, if you like, but you don't have to as they'll be covered in the final steps.

The image here shows the beauty of the frame that was hidden by the canvas. You can paint or stain the frame any color you like and set it aside for now. We'll work on the canvas for the next few steps.

Trimming your canvas can easily be done with a craft knife, scissors, or rotary cutter. Be sure to protect your fingers as you trim. Trim this to roughly the same size as your frame. I like to make mine a little smaller than the frame so the canvas won't hang over the edges when it is assembled.

Now that everything is disassembled, painted, and prepped, it's time to weed your cut iron-on design. I like to start by removing the large pieces and work my way inward, like the photo shows here.

When your weeding is complete, place the design in the middle of your trimmed canvas, as shown here.

For this next step, check the time/temperature settings for your particular material. I set my Cricut EasyPress to 340° for 30 seconds and applied light pressure during this process. Protect your workspace with a towel or heat pressing pillow.

Check if your material is a hot or cool peel and proceed as instructed. Peel off the carrier sheet to reveal your custom canvas.

The final step is assembly. I like to use a glue gun for this step and glue one edge at a time, working around the frame. Remember, you'll glue the canvas to the back of the frame, as shown here.

You can attach a bracket to the back of your frame, if you'd like to hang it on a wall, or display your new custom sign however you like.

MAKE IT **EXTRA**

This technique can be used with many different sizes of frames and can be customized with an endless array of colors and designs of your choosing. Have fun with it! These reverse canvases will look great in any room of your home and they can be lovely gifts with a sweet personalization. A gallery wall with a variety of designs would also make a great accent in any room!

Tumbler Decals

Adhesive vinyl decals can be added to nearly any smooth surface. A little decal can add a lot of cuteness to a set of tumblers, like I'll be showing you in this project. The key to this project is using both the positive and negative cuts from the vinyl: It's the ultimate way to stretch your materials and get two projects out of one cut. It's all in how you set up your project in Design Space. Ready? Let's do this!

Materials

Adhesive vinyl
Transfer tape
Tumblers (with a smooth surface for your decal)
Weeding tool
Scraper tool

Machine Compatibility

Any Cricut machine

DESIGN IT

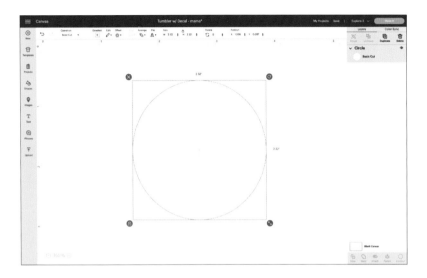

Measure your tumbler to see how much space you have to work with. The tumbler used in this project has a spot specifically for customization. Begin by choosing a shape for your overall decal; this specific tumbler calls for a circle that is sized it to 2.32″, as shown here.

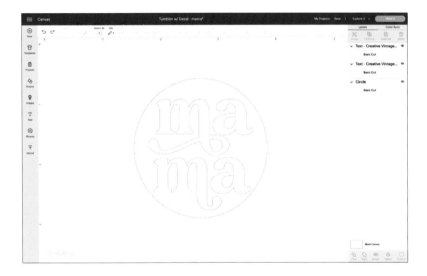

Next, add your text or image inside your shape. I've added some text and arranged it inside the circle. Make sure to leave a bit of space between your image and the outer edge of your shape. It's best to start with simple shapes until you become familiar with this process.

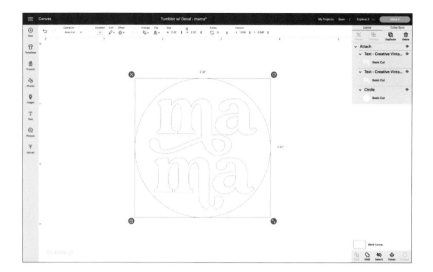

When your image/text is how you'd like it, select all the layers, and click on Attach. Your Cricut will cut your design exactly as it appears on the canvas, in a single layer.

MAKE IT

With these decals, the magic happens during the weeding process. From this single cut, you can utilize both the negative and positive areas. Before applying any vinyl, clean the tumbler's surface with rubbing alcohol to ensure good adhesion.

The only part of this cut that won't be used is the very outer area, so you can weed that part away but leave the rest.

Take a small piece of transfer tape, just a bit larger than your decal and gently lay it on top of your vinyl. Using your scraper tool, remove any air bubbles and make sure your vinyl is smooth and attached securely to your transfer tape.

PRO TIP
The transfer tape should be tacky, but not too tacky. If you notice your transfer tape is too tacky, you can tap it against your shirt or pants to make it a bit less sticky.

Gently peel away the transfer tape, but only remove the outer shape. Leave your image/text on the vinyl backing. Take your time and make sure not to rip the vinyl with any details your design may have. You can see in the image here that I only removed part of the vinyl as I lifted away the transfer tape.

Now that you have your isolated design on your transfer tape, place it onto your tumbler how you'd like it. First press the center of the decal down and then apply pressure working from the center to the outer edges, making sure to push out any bubbles that may be trapped.

After all the vinyl has been pressed down, use a scraper tool to make sure your vinyl is well adhered to your tumbler. Go over your decal gently, several times, with the transfer tape still attached.

Slowly pull the transfer tape away from the decal, pulling at an angle. If the vinyl seems to be pulling away with the transfer tape, you can use the scraper tool to ensure the vinyl stays put. Then try to peel again. Take your time until you get the hang of it.

After you've removed the transfer tape from your first tumbler, you can use that same transfer tape with the remaining decal that was left on the vinyl backing, as shown here.

Just as you applied the first decal, repeat the process on your second tumbler. Again, start by pressing down on the center of the decal and apply pressure outward. After the vinyl is fully adhered, gently remove the transfer tape at an angle.

Cheers! You now have a matching set of tumblers, one for you and one for a gift. Or keep them both for yourself. No judgment here!

MAKE IT **EXTRA**

This technique can be used with many different materials, by adding an outer shape you can create two projects from one cut. You can make besties shirts with iron-on material, multiple cards with the same cardstock design, or create more tumblers for you, your friends and family, or even for sale. Remember to peel your vinyl slowly to prevent ripping, and start with simple shapes and fonts until you're comfortable with more complex designs.

I love to use this technique with patterns like polka dots and polka hearts… that's a thing, right? But really, have fun and get creative!

Wooden Sign

Welcome! This is a great sign to hang on your front door. Your sentiment can be as welcoming or as snarky as you like since this project is so easily customizable. We'll be using stencil material for this project for a rustic painted look, but you could also use adhesive vinyl or iron-on vinyl to create your wooden sign.

Materials Needed

Stencil film/material (stencil film or removable vinyl)

Weeding tool

Blank wooden sign

Transfer tape/paper

Scraper tool/ squeegee

Painter's tape (optional)

Paint

Foam/paintbrush

Machine Compatibility

Explore or Maker series

Image Used

Botanical Wreath #M1803E971

DESIGN IT

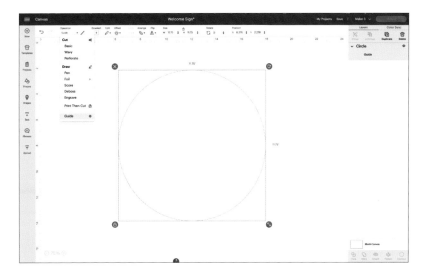

Before you start designing, measure your wood piece and then bring in a shape with the proper dimensions onto your Design Space canvas. First select your shape layer, and then on the Edit Bar in the Operation drop-down menu (where you find the Cut > Basic option), select Guide. This option will help you size your elements, but your machine will not cut this layer; it only serves as a template. My circle template is 11.75˝, as shown here.

Next, add some images and a bit of text. I went with a simple "welcome" and added a bit of fun with the glyphs of the letters. Size these new elements to fit inside your template from the previous step.

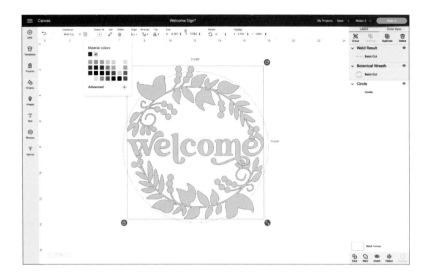

If you'll be using Stencil Film, it makes it easy if you change your elements to the same color, this will communicate to your Cricut that these elements will be cut from the same material.

After your design and/or text is finalized, click on the green Make It button.

MAKE IT

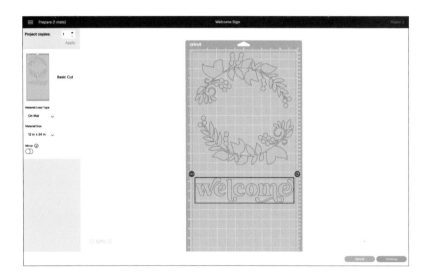

On the Make It screen you'll want to create some space between your images. Your images should have a border of at least 1″ so you have some room to work when painting. The less space you leave, the more careful you'll have to be when applying your paint. Simply select an image and drag it down a bit (it's also helpful if you center it, which makes the assembly process easier).

Once your material has been cut, weed your design. For this particular project, weed away any areas where you want to add paint. See the image here, which shows where to weed.

After you've completed weeding all your elements, cover your image with transfer tape. Make sure to eliminate any air bubbles by using a scraper tool/squeegee.

Once you've got your stencil pieces covered in transfer tape, apply the background design (in this case the floral wreath) to the wood round first, using what is called the hinge method. This is a great way to apply a medium- or large-sized decal or stencil. Begin by placing your stencil over your wood surface where you want it to be. Then take a piece of painter's tape and place it across the middle of your stencil and extend the tape on either side of the wood so it will stick to your worktable and keep your stencil in position, as shown in the image here. Being sure not to move your wood, peel back your stencil only as far as the painter's tape hinge.

Now that half of your stencil is exposed and pulled over the hinge, use your scissors and cut off the backing from that half of your stencil material.

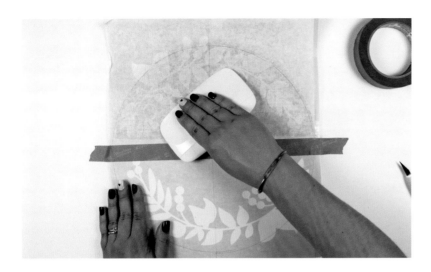

Place the stencil onto the wood and use the scraper tool/squeegee to make sure there are no air bubbles under your stencil.

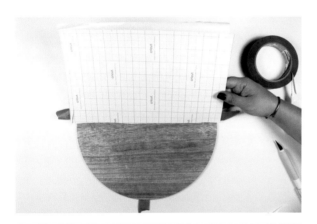

Repeat the same steps on the other half of your stencil: Lift your stencil up to the hinge; remove the stencil material backing; lay your stencil down and remove all the air bubbles using your scraper tool/squeegee.

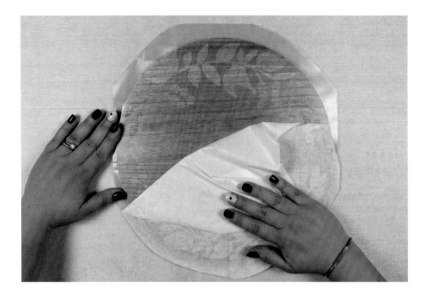

When all the air bubbles have been smoothed out, peel away the transfer tape. Make sure you don't lift or rip any pieces of your stencil material. Slow and steady wins the race. It is also helpful to pull back the transfer tape at a low angle.

Now that your stencil is in place and the transfer tape has been removed, it's time to apply your paint. You can use various types of paint on your stencils; just make sure it has a medium-thick consistency because thin paint tends to bleed under the stencil. Also, apply a small bit of paint to your brush at a time; you don't want to get too much paint in one spot as that can also bleed under your stencil.

PRO TIP
Tapping and dabbing motions are the way to go when applying paint; try not to use sweeping motions with your brush.

When you've allowed your paint to set for a few minutes, you can peel away the transfer tape. Some say to wait until the paint is fully dry, but you don't have to. I find that when the paint is too dry, it can pull away with the stencil.

Allow the first layer of paint to fully dry before moving on to the next steps.

To apply the next layer, use the hinge method again. Center your stencil and then place a piece of painter's tape down the middle of your stencil. Peel back half of your stencil and cut away the stencil material backing. Apply that half onto the wood and smooth out any air bubbles. Then repeat these steps for the other half of your design and then remove the transfer tape.

Again, apply the paint with a dabbing motion and when the paint has set for a few minutes, peel back the stencil. Make sure you don't get any paint from the stencil on your project, especially when weeding out the middles of your text/design.

The final step is applying whatever material you'd like to use for hanging your wood sign. Ribbon, wire, leather, or jute are great options.

MAKE IT **EXTRA**

Adding faux flowers, leaves, or stems to your stenciled sign is a great way to make it even more extra. You can even add bows, ribbons, or festive elements to really make your sign pop with personality!

CHAPTER TWO

Wearables

Your Cricut can create so much more than just decals and shirts. Within this chapter you can learn how to make stencils out of freezer-paper, different types of earrings, custom tote bags, headbands with faux leather bows, even a pair of crafty shoes! So many options of things to create…your imagination is your only limit. I truly hope the projects and tips in this chapter spark new ideas for you with what you have the ability and creativity to create.

Custom Crafty Shoes

Shoes are a great way to show off your unique style. With a little iron-on material and a handheld heat press you can create a pair of custom kicks for yourself, your friends, and your family.

Materials Needed

Shoes

Iron-on material (also known as heat transfer vinyl)

Weeding tool

Scissors/craft blade

Small/handheld heat press

Machine Compatibility

Any Cricut machine

Images Used

Paint Palette #M26273F27

Watercolor Paint #M2627FDB1

Crayons #M2627FD7B

Acrylic Paint Tube #M2627FDB8

Paint Brushes #M26273F24

Paint Brushes #M2627FD90

Scissors #M2627FDA7

Paint Tubes #M2627FD99

Glue Gun #M2627FD7E

DESIGN IT

You can customize your shoes with any design or pattern you can think up! For these shoes I am using the craft-themed images listed previously. Keep in mind when selecting your designs, they will need to be small as any fine details may be difficult to weed. You'll want to add all of your images to your canvas and then size them to be able to fit on your shoes. For these particular shoes I've sized each of the images to be no larger than 1.5″ x 1.5″.

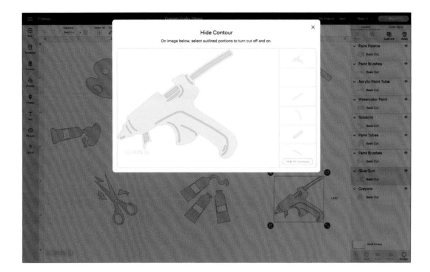

If your image has small details, the Contour tool is a great option for eliminating some of the unnecessary tiny cuts from your design. Clicking on the small sections removes them from the image.

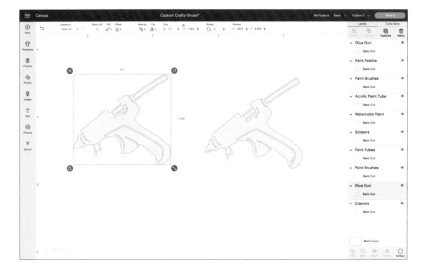

You'll be left with a design that still has the same outline shape and major details, but those fine details have been eliminated. This leaves a perfect image to be used on your shoes. In the image here, you can see the Glue Gun image on the left has had a small cut removed from the nozzle as well as the handle. The image on the right is the original file from Design Space. When this image is sized at 1.5″ across, the cuts that have been contoured out would be very intricate.

If you'd like to add variety to your design, you can duplicate the images and make them slightly larger or smaller.

MAKE IT

When on the Make It screen, double-check that you toggle the Mirror option, especially if your images have text. I would also suggest increasing the copies of your images on the Make It screen. This will allow you to cover your shoes with the designs and play with the layout.

When placing your material on the mat, put the shiny side down. There are a few instances where this isn't the case, but the majority of iron-on material is cut with the shiny side (carrier sheet) down. This will allow your machine to cut the material while keeping it attached to the clear carrier sheet.

Once your images are cut, slowly remove all the excess material around your design. I chose a reflective material for these shoes, just for fun!

When you've completed weeding it's a good idea to separate your designs, which will make applying them much easier. I used a craft blade for this part and it was quite a bit easier on the hands than using scissors.

Now that your images are separated, you can place them on your shoes however you like. Position them all on to make sure you like the layout before you set them with the heat press.

PRO TIP

If your pieces aren't sticking to your shoes, you can use heat resistant tape to keep them in place. When everything is in position the way you like, you can proceed to heat press one design at a time.

Check the instructions on your iron-on material to see if you should peel away the carrier sheet while it's still hot or if you should allow it to cool first. Peel as instructed.

Continue placing your designs on your shoes as shown here. If your designs are close together, as these are, press one at a time but wait to remove the carrier sheets until the whole area has been pressed.

MAKE IT **EXTRA**

Whether you're layering designs or incorporating specialty iron-on materials, you can be as creative as you'd like to show off your unique style. Using reflective iron-on, like I did, can add an element of safety to your shoes if you like to exercise or play during dusk or dawn. Another idea is to divide a larger image into two halves, and then place the right side of the design on one shoe and the left side of the design on the other shoe so that together, the two halves create a single design. This can assist children to learn which shoe goes on which foot and it can create a cool design for adults, too!

Earrings with Faux Leather

You're about to become hooked on making faux leather earrings! Faux leather earrings can be made using the techniques in this section and they can be customized to fit your personal aesthetic by using different shapes and colors. The best part is that faux leather is a lightweight material, making these earrings not only fun to wear but easy on the ears as well!

Materials Needed

Faux leather
Earring findings (jump rings and hooks)
Pliers
Jump ring opener tool

Machine Compatibility

Any Cricut machine

DESIGN IT

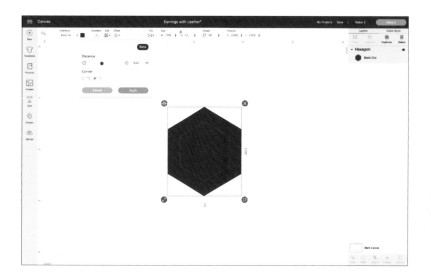

Begin with your basic shape on your canvas. For these earrings I went with a geometrical theme, so I started with a hexagon. I rotated the hexagon so that a corner would be at the top when assembled. Next, you will create an Inset, using the Offset tool. Enter −0.25″ into the designated box (as shown here) and select squared corners, not rounded. Then select Apply.

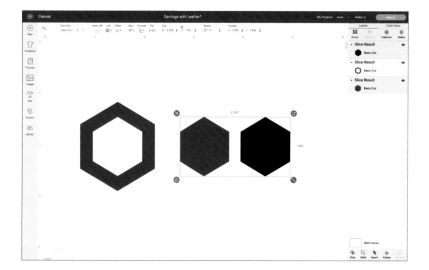

For the next step, you will select the original shape as well as the new inset layer and then click on Slice. This will create several layers we don't need on the canvas. The image here shows the two layers that need to be deleted.

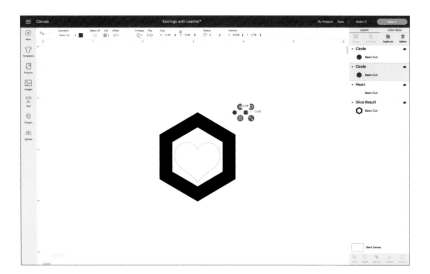

To create a level of fun and complexity I added a heart to these earrings, sized to float within the hollow hexagon. Also, two small circles sized .08″ have been added, which will be the holes for the jewelry hardware.

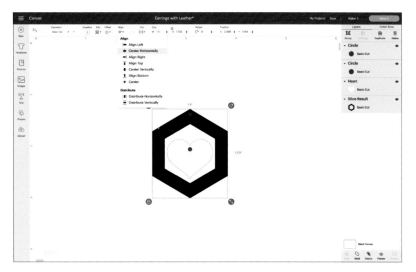

Drag these small circles onto the hexagon frame as well as the heart (or whatever shapes you've created). To make these perfectly centered, select all the layers and then click on Align > Center Horizontally, as shown here.

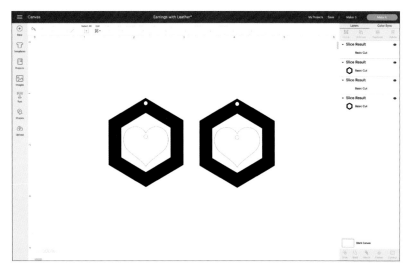

Select each shape and its corresponding small circle and then Slice. You'll then repeat this for your inner shape as well. Then remove any unwanted layers like the extra small circles that were created when sliced. Select all the layers and duplicate to make two earrings. Your canvas should resemble the image here. Now you're ready to click the green Make It button and cut your earrings.

MAKE IT

If your leather has a smooth side and a fuzzy side, place the smooth side against the mat. This will give you the cleanest cuts. Use a brayer to make sure the leather material is adhered well to your mat. I prefer to use a green mat for heavy materials like leather. On your machine, move the white star wheels on the metal bar to the far right, out of the way of your leather. Make small test cuts using different cut settings to ensure you have the right setting before cutting your whole project. Each type of leather has a different thickness/weight. I like to start with the Faux Leather setting which calls for the Fine-Point (normal blade), and you can add more pressure if necessary. If this setting, doesn't seem to be cutting through your leather, switch to the Genuine Leather setting and try various pressures until you find one that cuts cleanly through your material. The Genuine Leather setting calls for a Deep-Point Blade.

Once your material is cut, start opening your jump rings. I find it helpful to use two sets of pliers for this part, as shown here. You can also use a jump ring opener tool if you have one.

For these particular earrings, I used a large jump ring for the top hole in the hexagon. Through that same hole I inserted the earring hook. In the image here you can see that I added another smaller jump ring, which will connect to the small jump ring on the heart.

MAKE IT **EXTRA**

These earrings look great from any angle! The hearts float and swing inside the outer hexagon, which is already extra, but you could go further. These shapes could be swapped out to create a variety of styles. Adding additional jump rings is the key here. You could create even more elements by adding circles on the bottom of your shape and attaching more rings and shapes.

Earrings with Shrink Plastic

These unique earrings are a fun way to use shrink plastic, better known as Shrinky Dinks. You can create tons of custom earrings for yourself, your friends, or even to sell. These make great gifts when made with custom images and sayings.

Materials Needed

Shrink plastic/Shrinky Dink material
Color printer
Heat source (embossing gun or oven)
Earring findings (jump rings and hooks)
Pliers
Jump ring opener tool

Machine Compatibility

Maker or Explore series

Image Used

Heart Patch #MB6C10DC

DESIGN IT

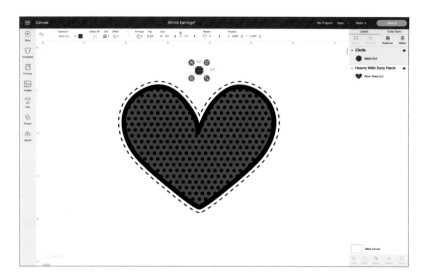

Start by selecting an image you'd like to turn into earrings and bringing it onto your canvas. Also add a small circle on your canvas, which will serve as the hole for the earring hook. Keep in mind that when using shrink materials your design will shrink roughly 300%. I sized these earrings to be 4″ when printed and they will be between 1.5″ and 1.75″ after heat is applied.

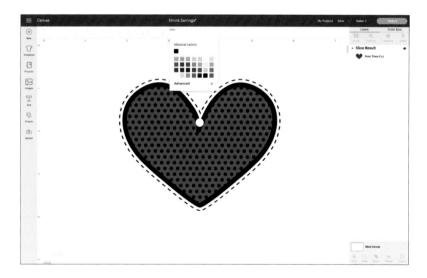

Next, move the small circle to the middle of your design, just a bit below the top edge. Select the small circle and your image layer and Slice. Then remove any extra small circle layers that have been created. You will keep just the main image that now has a hole in it.

PRO TIP

The design I chose has a white offset, which makes it difficult to see the edges of the design. Here is how to change the color of your canvas to remedy this. At the bottom of the Layers panel (when using a desktop/laptop) you'll see the words Blank Canvas next to a white rectangle. Your canvas is white as default; however, you can click on that white rectangle and then at the top of the screen you can select any color you'd like your canvas to be, as shown in the image above. This way you can see the edges of the design and can arrange accordingly.

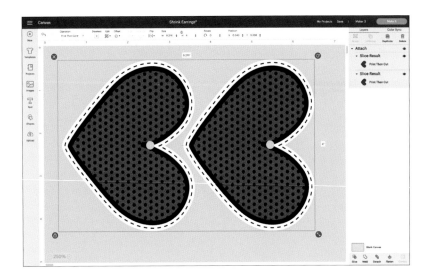

Duplicate your image and then click on Flip if you'd like your designs to be symmetrical. To make the best use of the material, I selected both layers and rotated 90°, and then I clicked on Attach. Make sure the combined width of your design does not exceed 6.75″, or a height of 9.25″, as this is the maximum Print Then Cut area.

MAKE IT

Send your design to your printer and print it on the shrink material. Then allow the printed shrink material to dry for several minutes before you place it onto your mat. The green mat is a great mat to use for shrink material. Use a brayer to make sure your shrink material is well adhered to your mat. The Acetate cut setting with More Pressure works for the shrink materials I have used, but to be sure it will work for your material too, do a small test cut before you begin cutting your whole project.

Once your cuts are finished remove any paper backing if your shrink material has any.

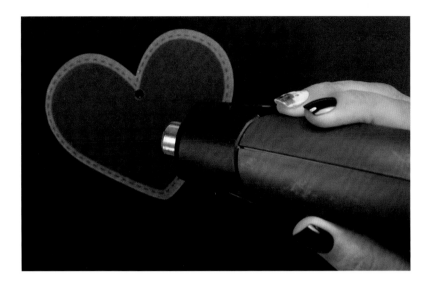

Now you're ready for the shrinking process, which can be done in an oven or with a heat gun. Check the instructions on your particular brand of shrinking material for heat time and temperature if you're using an oven. I used a heat gun for this project. Make sure your work surface is protected with heat safe materials.

Begin by swirling the heat gun around the surface of the shrink plastic.

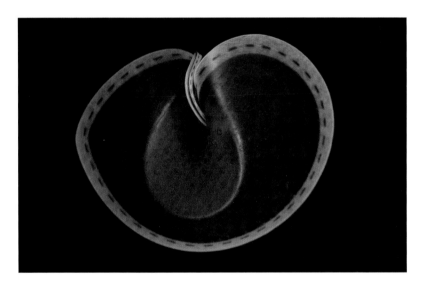

You will see the plastic start to melt and morph, which is a pretty cool process! Look at this picture here taken midway through the heating process. Don't worry; it will go back to being flat. If it doesn't, you can use tweezers or a heat safe tool to manipulate the material.

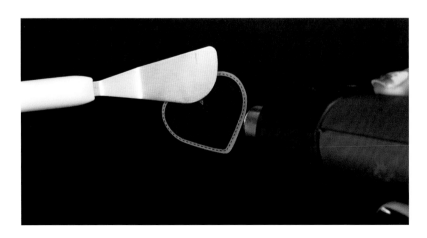

Toward the end of the process, you might need to help the material flatten completely as it cools. I use a little metal spatula to flatten the material, as shown here.

Here is a before and after photo. On the left the shrink material is 4″ wide; on the right it is roughly 1.5″ wide. After heating, the colors became more vibrant and the thickness of the material is about nine times thicker.

After your shrink material has cooled, grab your pliers and earring hardware to begin assembling your earrings. I used three jump rings for each earring, starting with the larger one closest to the heart. Feel free to make your earrings as long as you like or add any particular hardware you prefer.

MAKE IT **EXTRA**

Shrink material can be used in many different applications. You can use the techniques covered in this project to create charms for bracelets, necklaces, or even shoes! Attach a number of shrink designs on one earring just by creating more holes in the main shape and adding more jump rings. If you prefer the matte or shiny side of the earring facing out, and you're adding text, you can mirror the design so it prints backwards.

Headband with Faux Leather Bow

Create headbands for yourself or for the cuties in your life! This bow is a great beginner project, but it's impressive enough that your friends and family will exclaim, "You made that?" These bows can be sized for children or adults, and can be added to barrettes, earrings, keychains, or on a headband as taught in this section.

Materials Needed

Faux leather
Headband
Glue/adhesive (glue gun)

Machine Compatibility

Any Cricut machine

Image Used

Bow #M101F4A2C

DESIGN IT

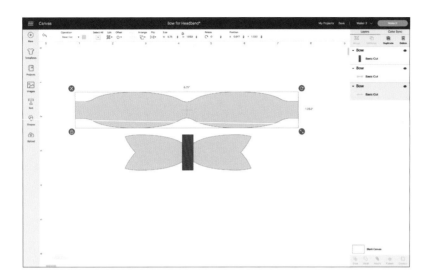

This is a quick and easy project and these bows can be used for many different applications. I started with image #M101F4A2C in Design Space, which is a basic two-layer bow with a middle piece to fasten it together.

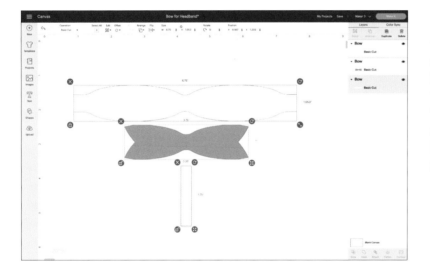

Feel free to adjust the size of the design to suit your creation. The dimensions for the bow that will be used within this project are shown here. When you've got your bow sized, click the green Make It button and read on to the next page.

MAKE IT

When cutting faux leather or genuine leather, place the material on the mat with the pattern/smooth surface facing down, as shown here.

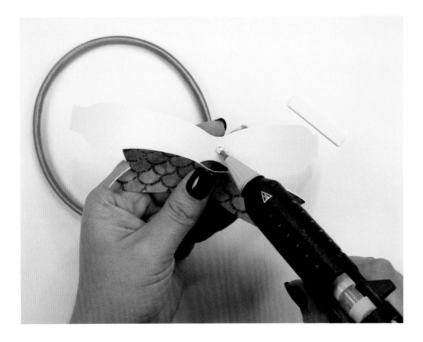

When prompted by Design Space to select your material, make sure to select Faux Leather. If you do not see it displayed, you can "Browse All Materials" (written in green) and select it from the list. For the standard Faux Leather setting, you will only need the Fine-Point Blade your machine came with.

Once you have your material cut, begin assembling your bow starting with the two larger pieces. A glue gun is a great option for assembling these bows.

Once the two main pieces have been glued together, flip it over to glue the underside of the bow.

Now it's time to add the piece that will wrap around the center of the bow and the headband. Start by centering it and gluing it to the top of the bow.

Continue to glue this piece around the bow and then wrap the pieces underneath the headband. Glue the ends to the headband, making sure everything is secure.

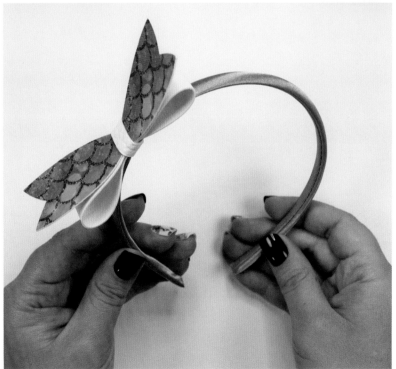

MAKE IT **EXTRA**

Now that you've made it once you can create bows for any occasion, in any size, and with any material. These bows would be adorable made of cardstock and put on top of a gift. You could also create larger bows and add them to a wreath or a sign. The options are endless!

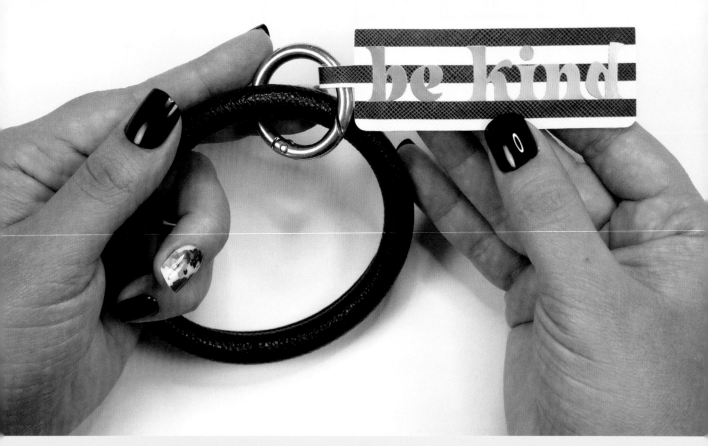

Leather Keychain with Iron-On

A custom keychain can be a great gift for a loved one or make one (or more) for yourself! For this project I made a gentle reminder to "be kind" on the road. These creations can be customized using different patterns of faux leather and can be adorned with your favorite iron-on material.

Materials Needed

Faux or genuine leather
Iron-on material
Heat source (iron or heat press)
Keychain hardware

Machine Compatibility

Any Cricut machine

Image Used

Rectangular Label #M38719

DESIGN IT

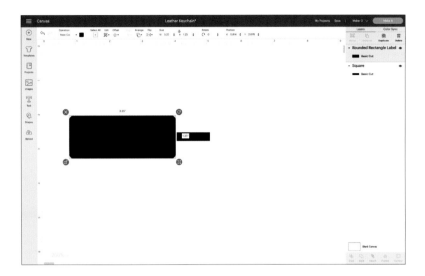

For this leather keychain, start by selecting basic shapes and bringing them onto your canvas. This Rounded Rectangle image makes for a great universal shape. Also add a normal rectangle sized 1˝ × .25˝, which will be the connector piece between the front and back of the keychain. See the image here and compare it to your canvas.

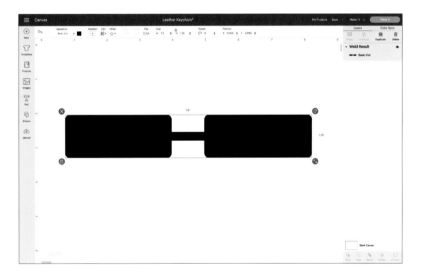

Duplicate the larger rectangle and space them out with all the ends touching. Select all the layers and then select Align > Center Vertically. When your shapes are aligned, make sure everything is still selected and click Weld. Your canvas should look similar to the image here.

Add any text or additional images you'd like on your keychain. Size proportionally and change the colors of the layers so your machine will recognize that you are cutting different materials. In the image here, the black layers will be cut from faux leather and the yellow layer will be cut from a metallic iron-on material.

MAKE IT

When cutting your materials, you can choose a different cut setting for each mat. Reminder: Toggle the Mirror setting for any iron-on images and text. When you cut iron-on material, you almost always cut with the shiny side facing the mat. There are instances, like patterned iron-on, where you don't do it that way, but best practice is to place the shiny side down and mirror your designs. You will also place your leather with the pattern/smooth side facing the mat, as shown here.

After all your pieces are cut, you need to weed your iron-on. Remove every piece of material, except for your final design. Remember to check the insides of your letters or images.

The Cricut EasyPress Mini is a great tool to use for tiny applications like this keychain. Be sure to check your material's instructions for specific temperature and time.

It's a good idea to protect your faux leather with parchment paper or a Teflon sheet as you heat press.

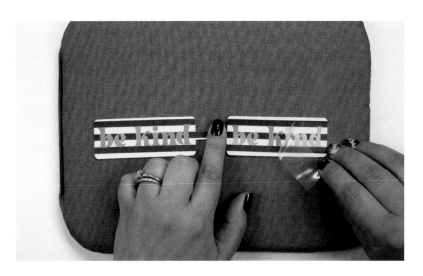

After you've heat pressed your keychain, it's time to remove the carrier sheet. Each material is different, and some suggest peeling the carrier sheet while it's still warm, while others suggest a cool peel. If you peel at the wrong time, it could lift your iron-on material and ruin your design. Be patient if you have a cool peel material— you'll be glad you were!

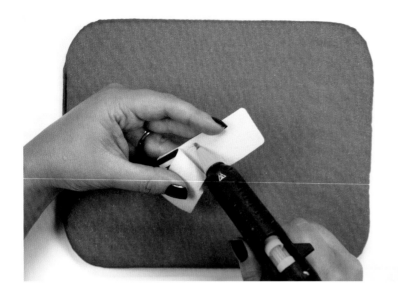

Now it's time to fold your keychain in half and glue it together. You can use your favorite fabric glue or even a glue gun using glue sticks made especially for fabric. If you're working with a glue gun, keep in mind the glue will be warm and tacky for only a few seconds, so work in small sections.

If you're using a glue gun, you won't have to wait long for your glue to dry. If you're using liquid glue, you might want to use binder clips to hold your leather in place as it dries.

MAKE IT **EXTRA**

You can mix and and match different iron-on materials and faux leather colors, patterns and shapes to create a wide variety of custom keychains. So many options! You could even enlarge this design and make tags for Christmas stockings or make them small for gift tags. I paired my keychain with a matching leather tassel. If you'd like to do the same, you can find the full instructions in the following section.

Leather Tassel for Keychain

This easy-to-make tassel is a fun addition to your keychain but can be used for so much more! I've listed several out-of-the box ideas in the "Make It Extra" section of this project. Have fun with different color combinations and faux leather patterns. I put my tassel on my keychain and I love it!

Materials Needed

Faux leather or genuine leather
Glue/adhesive
Keychain hardware

Machine Compatibility

Any Cricut machine (if using faux leather)

Ready to Make Project

Leather Tassel Keychain

DESIGN IT

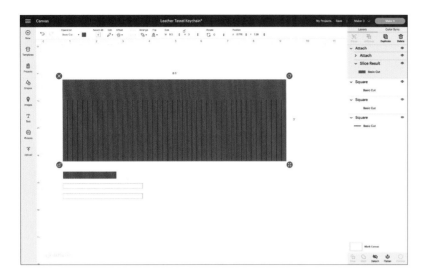

These tassels make a fun addition to a keychain or zipper pull, just to name a few possible applications. In Design Space, click the Projects tab and search for the project "Leather Tassel Keychain" and select Customize. Here you can change the size and colors of your desired keychain. The image here shows the sizes used for this project.

You can design your tassel to have a longer or shorter fringe. Just select the layer you'd like to resize and click the Unlock icon in the lower-left corner of the image. Now you can freely adjust the proportions and size of your shape.

MAKE IT

Whether you're using faux leather or genuine leather, you'll want the smooth side of your material to face down on the mat. Use a brayer to make sure your material is well adhered.

After your materials are cut, run your fingers through the fringe to make sure they are all separated.

First, glue the small rectangle to the larger piece of faux leather. This will be the loop that attaches your tassel to your keychain. Fold the rectangle in half and glue near the edge of your larger piece of material, as shown here.

Roll the material lengthwise and glue in small sections as you wrap.

After you've completed rolling and gluing the tassel, glue the smaller accent strips to the top of the tassel. While this step isn't necessary, it sure does add a bit of fun to your hand-made tassel.

This tassel can simply be added to your keychain or paired with another hand-made keychain. Instructions for this matching "Be Kind" keychain can be found in the previous section.

MAKE IT **EXTRA**

These tassels are so versatile. They can be used not only as a keychain, but they can be added to a purse, backpack, or sweatshirt. You could even resize them and use them as home décor for a ceiling fan chain, light pulls, or dresser drawer handles. Have fun with different sizes, patterns, and colors!

Shirt With Freezer Paper Stencil

Create a new custom shirt with a vintage feel! For this project, freezer paper and an upcycled carrier sheet are the heroes. A carrier sheet is the clear backing you peel when working with traditional iron-on. Don't throw those out! You can reuse them for projects like this and more.

Materials Needed

Freezer paper
Used carrier sheet (clear backing from previous iron-on project)
Brayer
Sponge or foam brush
Acrylic paint or screen-printing ink
Paint tray/palette
Heat source (iron or heat press)

Machine Compatibility

Maker or Explore series

DESIGN IT

The magic in this project is all about the technique! It will work best if you keep your design and/or font simple. See here for an example of a flourished font, but still keeping it simple.

Adjusting the layout and the spacing (kerning) of the font is a great way to take simple text and turn it into a design. The image here is an example of what a little adjustment can do. When your image is exactly how you want it to be on your shirt, select all the layers and then click Attach. This will communicate to your Cricut that everything will be cut on one layer, just as it is shown on your canvas.

MAKE IT

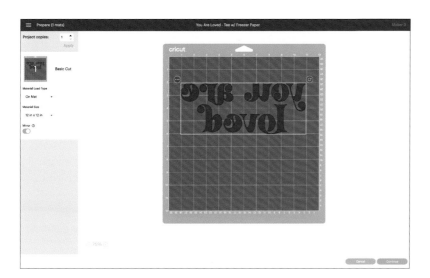

When you are on the Make It screen, Mirror your image/text and also drag your image to the center of the mat. This will create a border for your stencil, as shown here.

You can repurpose/reuse an old carrier sheet for this project (the clear plastic backing from iron-on material). Whenever I complete a large iron-on design, I save the carrier sheet and have collected a small stash of them for projects just like this.

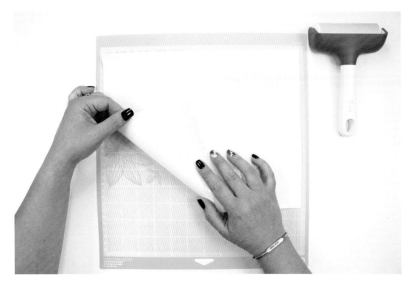

Tear off a piece of freezer paper approximately the same size as your carrier sheet (which should be a little bit bigger than your final design). Use a brayer and roll the freezer paper onto the carrier sheet, making sure the shiny side of the freezer paper is facing up. The brayer will help remove any bubbles between the carrier sheet and freezer paper; you may need to roll over it several times. Trim off any excess freezer paper.

Now, take the freezer paper attached to the carrier sheet and place it onto the mat with the carrier sheet facing down (on the mat). The brayer will come in handy again to roll the materials onto the mat to eliminate any air pockets between your materials and the mat.

When cutting this material, you can select the Iron-On setting and you should get clean cuts. If your cuts are not coming out clean, you can play with some custom pressure settings.

While your design is still on the mat, weed away your design, like the image here. Usually, you would weed away all the material around your design, but for stencils, you instead remove only the actual design and leave the surrounding material. The reason for leaving your material on the mat is it might curl and loosen if you remove it before weeding.

PRO TIP

To remove your material from your mat, flip your mat over and gently roll the mat away from your material, as shown here. This will help any small pieces stay where they need to be.

Now, this is when the carrier sheet comes in handy. Instead of having to place your freezer paper piece by piece onto your shirt, you can just place the whole sheet where you want your design. To turn this into a paintable stencil, you will heat press your design and carrier sheet at 310° for 5 seconds, slowly moving the heat press around your design to make sure every spot has been evenly heated. When the carrier sheet has cooled, peel it back to uncover your freezer paper stencil. If there are sections of your freezer paper that haven't adhered to your shirt, you can heat it again for a few seconds.

Use acrylic paint or screen-printing ink to fill your design. A gentle pouncing motion with a foam brush or sponge will give the best result. Avoid moving the brush side to side, as it will lift the freezer paper.

When your paint/ink has dried, peel back the freezer paper to reveal your design, like the image here. Tweezers come in handy when removing small pieces.

Allow your design to dry overnight and then heat-set it. You can use an iron or a heat press to do this. If using a heat press, set it to 320° for 40 seconds. This will help your design to maintain permanence wash after wash.

MAKE IT **EXTRA**

The main difference between this technique and using iron-on material is the effect you get by sponging on the paint, which gives a vintage look. You can use as many paint/ink colors as you like. An ombre or rainbow colors would make your design really pop! Small sponges can be used to create fine detail for different parts of your designs. You could also create a design that would normally use several colors of iron-on but cut them as a single layer, and then hand-paint the design. So many options are possible with this technique. I'd love to see what you create! The next time you do an iron-on project, don't throw out your carrier sheet. Reduce, reuse, re…craft!

Tote Bag with Iron-On

Can you ever have too many bags? Whether you are going to the beach or park, or you're grocery shopping with reusable bags, a custom tote is always useful! Tote bags can be easily customized, and they make for a great keepsake for a girls' weekend, bridal party, or just because!

Materials Needed

Iron-on material (also known as heat transfer vinyl)
Blank tote bag
Weeding tool
Heat press

Machine Compatibility

Any Cricut machine (depending on the design size)

Image Used

Globe with Flowers #M27FB59AC

DESIGN IT

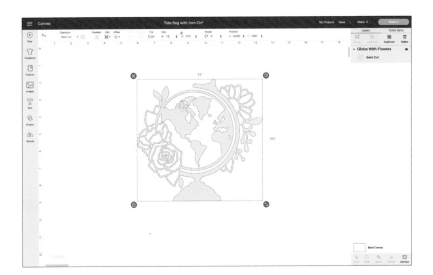

Start by adding your chosen design to your canvas. I used this gorgeous globe.

Add a bit of text to your design to personalize it. Select both layers and then select Align > Center Horizontally, as shown here. When your image is how you want it to look on your tote bag, select all the layers and click on Attach. This will keep your designs in place when you cut them.

MAKE IT

When you cut iron-on material, you will need to Mirror your design on the Make It screen. Make sure your material is placed with the shiny side facing down on your mat. There are exceptions to this rule, but shiny side down is almost always the case.

After you have completed cutting your design, remove from the mat and weed away any material that is not part of your design. I like to start with the larger pieces, like the background, and work my way toward the center; but the more you weed, you will find your groove and can go with what is most practical to you.

Center your weeded design on your tote bag. You can eyeball it or use a ruler to make sure it's just right.

Once your image is placed exactly where you want it, it's time to use the heat press. Find the heat temperature and time instructions for the particular material you are using. Not all materials are created equal. For this material, I'll be heat pressing at 305° for 30 seconds.

The material used here calls for a cool peel. Most materials will specify if it's a warm or cool peel so be sure to check your directions: This part does matter! If you peel too soon, your design might lift with the carrier sheet, ruining your design. The peeling part may be the most satisfying step of this whole process.

MAKE IT **EXTRA**

Iron-on can be used on a variety of items. Typically, iron-on material is used for apparel, but did you know you can also use iron-on with wood, leather, canvas, and ceramic? Part of the fun is experimenting with your craft. Adding layers and different styles of iron-on can make any project extra fancy. Adding elements of glitter, foil, holographic finishes, mosaic patterns, or any number of iron-on materials can take your project to the next level.

CHAPTER THREE

DIY Gifting

Cards, gift tags, stamps, oh my! Make your special someone feel even more special when you create any of the items in this chapter for them. Go all out and make personalized wrapping paper, gift tags, a shaker or spinning card, and a matching envelope. Whether you create all these things, or just pick and choose, your sweet gesture is sure to be met with smiles and twinkly eyes. The craft projects to follow can easily be transformed to meet your party and holiday needs. Have fun and don't be afraid to Make It Extra!

Foam Stamps

Did you know you can make your own stamps with your Cricut? You can, and it's so fun! You can create custom stamps to use on cards, envelopes, or even to create your own gift wrap. So many possibilities!

Materials Needed

Craft foam (with adhesive backing for best results)

Wooden blocks (large and flat work best)

Tweezers

Glue/adhesive with fine tip applicator (optional)

Blank wrapping paper

Knife Blade for Maker machine (best results) or Deep-Point Blade for Explore Air 2 machine

Machine Compatibility

Maker or Explore series

Images Used

Streamers and Confetti #M3A179

Cake on Stand #M2841CC1E

DESIGN IT

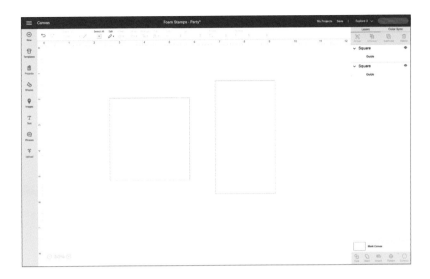

To make your stamps, first measure the surface of your wood block. On your canvas create a square/rectangle the size of your wood-block surface. Then turn those shapes into Guides from the Operation drop down menu.

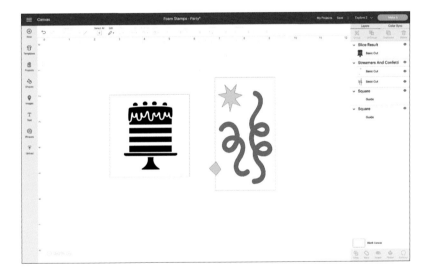

Next, bring your images onto your canvas and size them to fit within your guide shapes. Your canvas may look something like the image here. Notice how the Streamers and Confetti image is outside my guideline just a bit. We'll play with that part in a few steps.

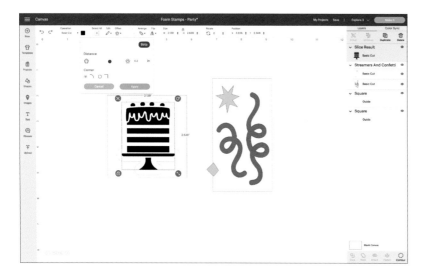

We'll make these stamps two different ways. Let's work with the Cake on Stand stamp first. Select the Cake on Stand image and create an offset. The image here has a 0.20″ offset.

Duplicate the offset layer you just created. Then select one of the offset layers, and the Cake on Stand layer, and then Slice. Remove the initial image layer as well as one of the sliced offset layers, keeping only the sliced result and an offset layer, as shown here. These duplicated layers will make your stamps have a bit of depth on the wood blocks.

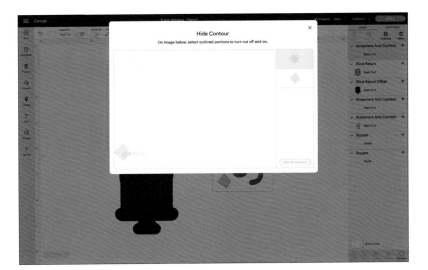

Let's move over to the Streamers and Confetti stamp. You may notice that the image has two different layers. Ungroup this image and resize it so the image fills your Guide. Just for fun you can duplicate the confetti layer and use the Contour tool to remove the star shape as shown in the image on the left.

From here you can play with the arrangement of your images within your Guides, and then Attach and Duplicate the images for this stamp.

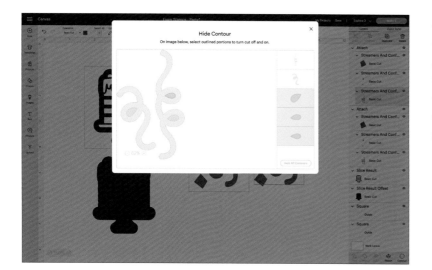

To increase the stability of this image, Contour the centers of the streamers out of the image, as shown here. Do this for only one of the layers, this will be your base during the assembly process.

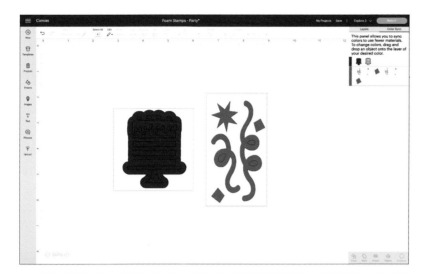

Align all your layers so you have a good visualization of what they will look like assembled. To cut all the images from the same piece of craft foam, change the layers to the same color. The easiest way to do that is by using the Color Sync tool at the top of the layers panel. Simply drag and drop the images from the dark-gray box into the purple box. Isn't that neat? Now all your layers are the same color.

Click on the green Make It button to send it to the mat.

MAKE IT

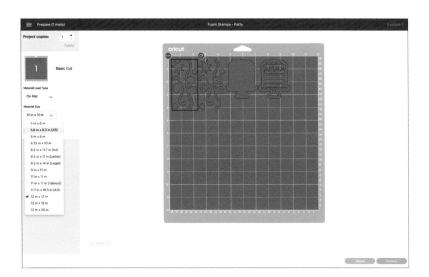

On the Make It screen you have the option to change your material size. The adhesive craft foam used in this project is 6″ × 9″. The closest option to those measurements found in the drop-down menu is 5.8″ × 8.3″, which is pretty close. You can also use this feature if you're ever cutting other materials like 8.5″ × 11″ cardstock or copy paper.

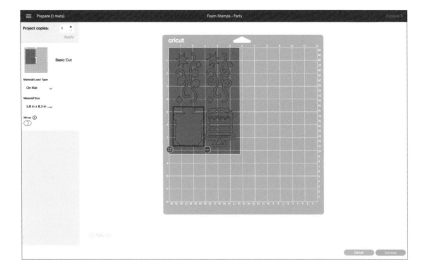

Arrange your images within the mat, making sure to leave room around the edges. You can even rotate your images to make the most out of the material you're using.

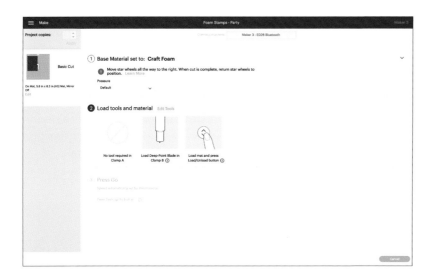

Once you select Craft Foam from your list of materials, look for the option that says Edit Tools (right next to Load tools and material). This is where you'll select Knife Blade if you're using a Cricut Maker.

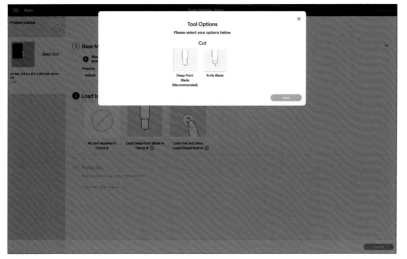

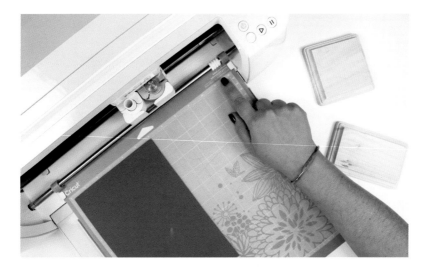

Before you load your mat, check that your star wheels are moved all the way to the right on the bar, like the photo here. Also, load your Knife Blade into your machine, or the Deep-Point Blade if you're using an Explore machine.

When your cuts are complete, remove the craft foam from your mat. If you're using adhesive craft foam (suggested) keep the paper backing intact. Carefully weed away the negative space around your designs and also the inner details of the foam. Tweezers are a great tool for this.

Here's where the adhesive craft foam comes in handy. Simply place the contoured images onto your wooden blocks. If you're working with non-adhesive craft foam, use a fine-tipped glue applicator for these next few steps.

For the second layer, which has the details, you can either peel the whole design away from the foam backing or pull back a bit at a time while applying it.

The streamers and confetti with the thinner foam cuts can be applied with tweezers. Place the contoured layer of foam down first, the one that doesn't have any of the inner details. Carefully line up the layers when placing the second layer of foam.

Now that your stamps are complete, you can begin to roll out your plain wrapping paper, grab your stamp pads, and stamp away. If you used glue during the application process, make sure the glue is dry before you use your stamps.

MAKE IT **EXTRA**

Making custom stamps is already a bit extra, but think of all the things you could do with this idea. You can create teachers' gifts or special stamps for each person's gift wrap throughout the year for birthdays and holidays. Even a simple to-and-from stamp would add a special touch to any gift!

Foiled Gift Tags

A custom gift tag can be added to any gift, or perhaps you've already made the personalized gift wrap from this chapter and you're looking for that perfect matching gift tag. These sparkly tags will give any gift that special, crafty, personalized touch. This is a great project to get comfortable with the Foil Transfer Tool, too!

Materials

Cardstock
Foil Transfer Tool
Foil Transfer Sheets
Washi or painter's tape
Ribbon

Machine Compatibility

Any Cricut machine

Images Used

Rounded Gift Tag #M2AAB3E66
Cake on Stand #M2841CC1E
Oval #M2AAB3D97

DESIGN IT

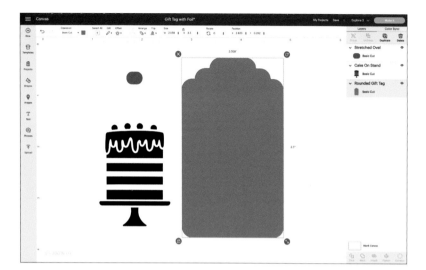

Begin by bringing the images you'll use onto your canvas.

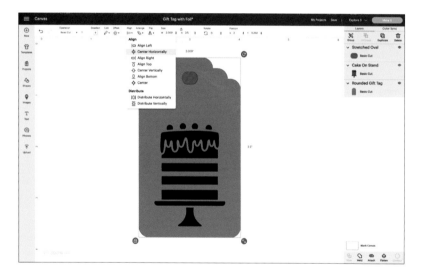

Next, arrange your images and make sure to leave some room for text. Select all the layers and select Align > Center Horizontally to ensure everything is centered on your gift tag.

Now let's add some text. Use the Filter option in the Text box and check the Writing box. This will provide you with all the options for the best font to use. Your Cricut machine writes by outlining the font, unless the font is labeled as a Writing font. Keep that in mind when selecting your font.

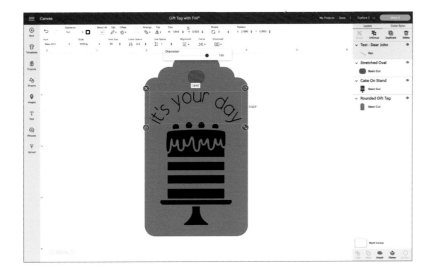

Size your text so it stretches across your gift tag with a small border on either side, then select the Curve text option. Play with what looks good to you. Using the Letter Spacing function can also help when adjusting your curved text.

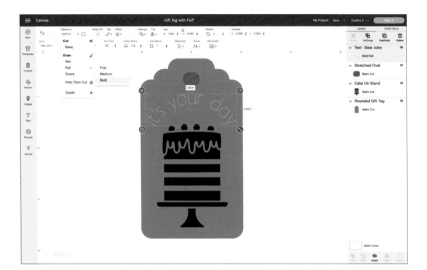

When your text is the way you want it to be, change the Operation to Foil and choose your Tip option and color.

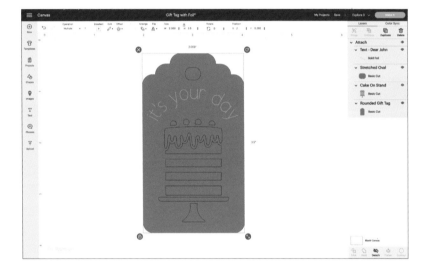

The final step before sending your project to the mat is to select everything, then Attach. Click the green Make It button.

MAKE IT

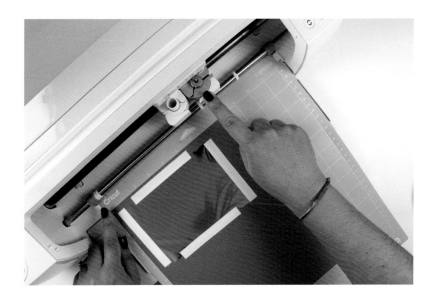

The Foil Transfer Tool process is a bit different than just cutting your material straightaway. You'll need to start by laying the foil over your cardstock. Using the tape that comes with the Foil Transfer Sheets (washi or painters tape), make sure you tape all four edges of the foil down. Try and make the foil as smooth and secure as you can because if it's not taped well, your foil will shift.

Before you start your machine, swap out your Fine-Point Blade for the Bold Foil Transfer Tip (the one with three lines). When this first process is complete, remove the foil but do not unload your mat yet. Just slide the foil out from underneath the carriage and set it to the side so you can make your gift tags extra (more on that in a bit). At this time swap out the Foil Transfer Tip for your Fine-Point Blade.

When the cutting process is complete, all you need to do is remove your gift tags from the mat and add your ribbon. Remember to flip the mat over and roll away the mat from your cardstock, which will prevent your cardstock from curling.

MAKE IT **EXTRA**

Grab that foil you put aside when you removed it from the cardstock and cut a piece slightly larger than your cut-out image. Using double-sided tape or fine-tipped glue, adhere the foil to the back of your gift tag. You will be able to see the trimmed foil piece from the other side, but you can easily cover it up with another gift tag to make a two-sided tag, or just leave it. Now you have a foil peek-a-boo gift tag. So pretty!

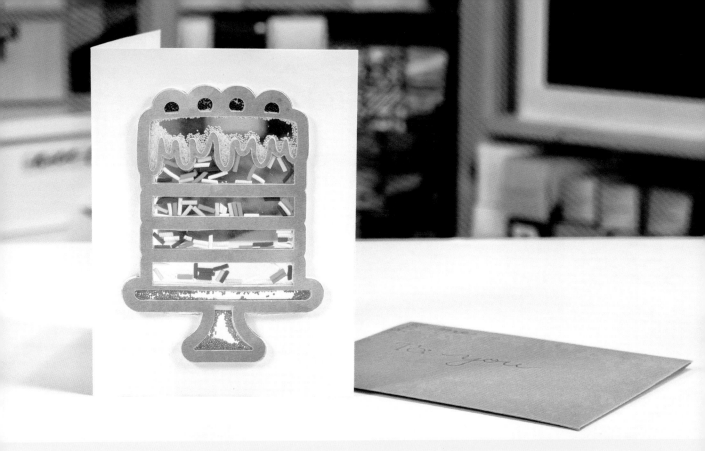

Transparent Shaker Card

Add a little fun and whimsy to your handmade cards: Make 'em shake! In the Let's Party chapter, you might have seen the sections on Shaker Cake Toppers and Cupcake Toppers. This would be a perfect pairing for those special decorations. Although this project is made with a cake design, you could create a shaker card with any image you like…as long as it's got room to shake!

Materials Needed

Cardstock

Acetate

Glue

Glitter and/or shaker bits (beads/sequins)

Craft foam (with adhesive backing for best results)

Knife Blade for Maker machine (best results) or Deep-Point Blade for Explore Air 2 machine

Machine Compatibility

Maker or Explore series

Image Used

Cake on Stand #M2841CC1E

DESIGN IT

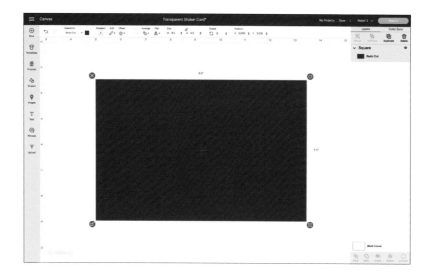

Start with a blank canvas and add your open card shape. The final card will be 4.25″ × 5.5″ so try to visualize an open card with the measurements 8.5″ × 5.5″, as shown in the image here.

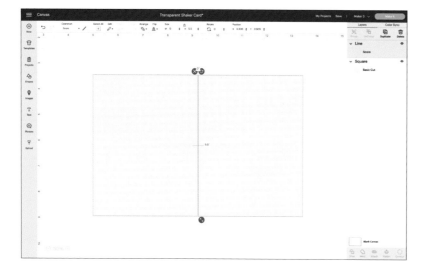

Next, add a score line to your canvas. You'll find this when you open the Shapes tab; it's the thin line (the first shape listed in the upper left). Once the line appears on your canvas, make sure that the Operation is set to Score. Also change the height of the score line to 5.5″ and Align > Center to your full card shape. I also changed the color of the card here so you can clearly see the score line in the center.

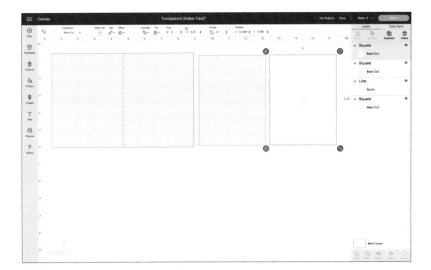

While you're making rectangles, make one more that is 4″ × 5.25″ and then duplicate it. Change the colors of these layers: one to match the card and one to resemble the acetate backing layer.

PRO TIP
Acetate is a clear plastic material that will make your shaker transparent and unique. I like to use a very light-blue color for these layers (as shown here), but you can use whatever color you'd like—as long as you remember what color each layer needs to be when it comes time for your cuts.

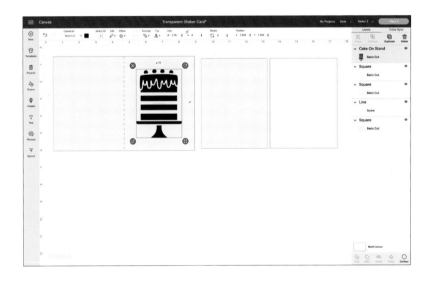

Now let's bring in the image for the shaker. This Cake on Stand image will make a fun and festive card. Bonus for matching all the other projects in this section! Add the image to your canvas and then size and center it, leaving a bit of room around each edge of the card, like the image here.

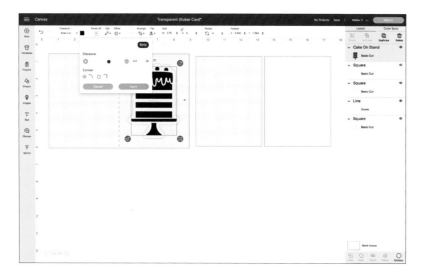

Next, make an Offset of the Cake on Stand image. I'd suggest an offset of at least 0.20˝.

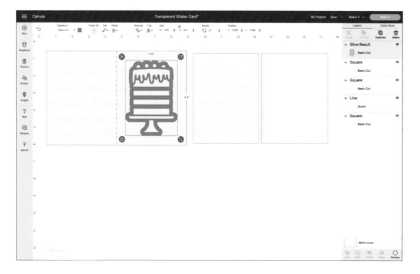

Now select your new offset layer and the original Cake on Stand image and Slice. Then delete the excess layers and you'll be left with a canvas that resembles the image here. This new layer will be your foam layer. It may help to keep things organized if you change this layer color to the same color as the foam you will use.

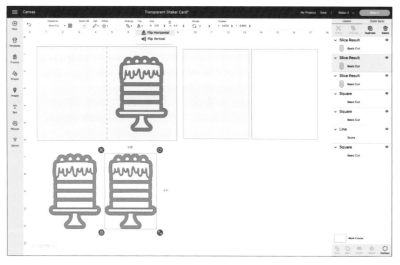

Duplicate your foam layer two times to use for cardstock accent pieces. These will be used as fun cardstock that will cover any visible foam and/or glue. Change the color of these layers to resemble the cardstock you've chosen as your accent. Also, Flip one of these layers. This reversed layer will be used to hide the back of your foam. You'll find more details on how to create the shaker assembly in the "Make It" section here.

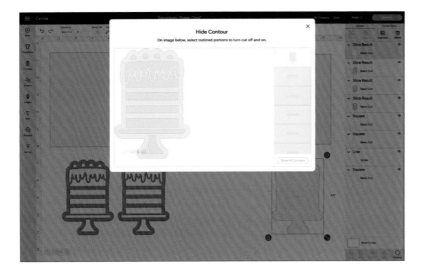

Alright, there are just a few more elements to make. Duplicate the sliced Cake on Stand image one more time to use for a second acetate layer. As is, this won't keep any shaker pieces in, so we need to use the Contour tool and Hide All Contours, as shown here. After contouring this layer, change it to the same color you have your other acetate layer, shown here in light blue (behind the contour box). You might notice this looks the same as the initial offset layer, which could have just been duplicated, but I wanted to show you the image-editing steps within Design Space.

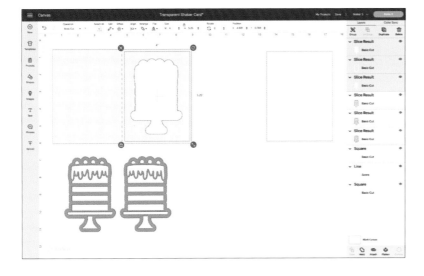

Now we need to turn this into a transparent card. To do this, bring the inner-card backing layer (same color as your card) and the acetate layer you just made and put them over the full card layer. Line up these elements to the foam layer that is already there. Select the acetate layer and inner-card backing layer and then Slice. You've just created new layers. You can get rid of these new layers in a minute but right now don't move anything—keep everything where it is for the next step.

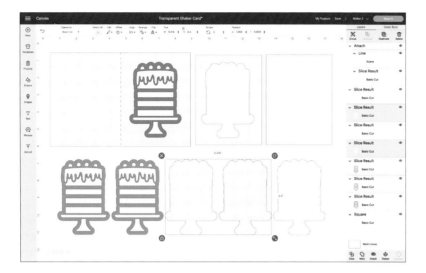

Next, select the full card layer and the acetate layer you just worked with and Slice. Notice that editing with these layers has pushed the score line to the back of the canvas. Select the score line and click Arrange, then Bring to Front. Then select the score line and the full card layer and Attach. Your Layers panel should look similar to the image here. I separated all the layers so you can easily see what should be there. See those two layers of cake selected in the bottom row (the same color as the cardstock)? Delete those two layers.

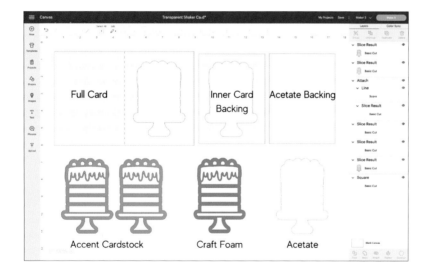

Before you send your project to the mat, make sure your Layers panel resembles the image here. Use this image as your guide for when you Make It. I hope it helps organize your layers during assembly. Now you are ready to click the green Make It button.

MAKE IT

Use a craft foam that has an adhesive backing, which makes for a much smoother process, rather than having to wait for wet glue to dry on both sides of the foam. It also helps to eliminate any of your shaker elements from adhering to excess glue. When cutting your craft foam, the Knife Blade in the Maker will give you the best results, though it is possible to cut using the Deep-Point Blade. Tweezers are a great tool for weeding foam.

PRO TIP

Acetate can have a static charge to it. To reduce any static, you can gently swipe both sides of the acetate with a dryer sheet before or after cutting. You can also clean acetate with dish soap and water. Glitter and other small particles tend to stick to acetate, so this process will help cut back on that and will leave your shaker looking clean and professional.

I recommend using a brayer to remove air bubbles when placing your acetate material onto your mat. Most acetate has a protective plastic liner on one side, so be sure you remove the liner before applying your material to your mat.

Now that your layers have been cut and prepped, follow this order of assembly to create your shaker cake topper.

From the front of the card to the middle:

» Accent cardstock
» Acetate
» Craft foam
» Full card
» Acetate backing
» Inner-card backing
» Inner-accent cardstock

Start by adhering your foam layer and cake-shaped acetate. Adhesive craft foam makes this step very easy and mess-free. If you're using glue, wait until your glue dries before moving on to the next steps.

Now comes the fun part of filling each little pocket with glitter and shaker bits. These cute little sprinkles made of polymer clay make a perfect addition to a cake shaker. You can put the same kind of shaker elements into each section or switch it up and add variety.

Carefully set your filled foam aside. Grab the inner-card backing and the acetate backing and glue these pieces together.

Back to the shaker. Apply a thin line of glue along the exposed foam. Taking the piece of acetate and cardstock from the previous step, acetate side facing down, carefully line up the edges of the foam with the cutout of the cardstock. This step is shown in the image to the left. Make sure there are no gaps in the glue, which will ensure your glitter and shaker bits don't fall out once fully assembled. Set this aside to dry before moving on.

PRO TIP
A fine-tipped glue applicator is recommended for projects like these where you want to avoid any pooling of adhesives. Important: Even though you will be tempted to shake that shaker the moment you put it all together, allow the glue to dry first.

When the pieces you just glued are dry, grab the matching accent cardstock piece and glue it to the exposed foam. Line this up to where the edge of the cardstock meets the foam, as shown here.

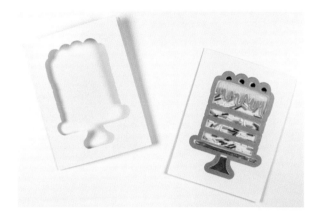

We will now move on to the front of the card. Open your card and apply glue along the inside. Then nest the other assembled piece within the cutout of the card.

For the final step, apply the last piece of accent cardstock to the front of the card. Again, apply a thin bead of glue and line up your pieces to cover the foam.

When all the pieces have dried, shake it baby, shake it!

MAKE IT **EXTRA**

Admittedly, shaker cards are already a bit extra, but if you'd like to go even further, you can add more embellishments inside the shaker that are small enough and will shake and add excitement. You can also add extra layers for more dimension. If you're looking for a matching envelope for your new shaker card, check the Envelope project (found later in this section). So cute!

Spinning Card

This card has a bit of magic in it. Not only does the cake look like it's levitating, but it can also spin! When gifting these cards, I recommend twisting the cake a few times before placing it inside an envelope. When the recipient opens the card, the cake will spin. So fun!

Materials Needed

Cardstock

Sticker cardstock (optional)

Fishing line

Holographic vinyl

Transfer tape

Scissors

Glue/adhesive

Weeding tool

Machine Compatibility

Any Cricut machine

Image Used

Cake on Stand #M2841CC1E

DESIGN IT

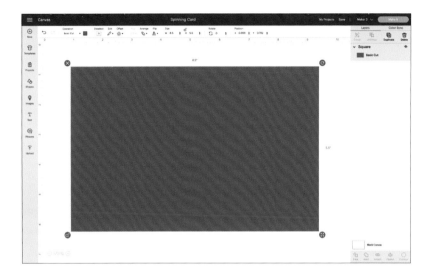

Start with a blank canvas and add your open card shape. The final (folded) card will be 4.25″ × 5.5″ so the open card will measure 8.5″ × 5.5″, as shown in the image here.

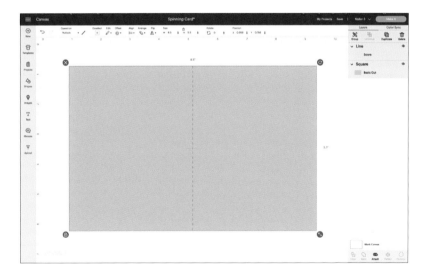

Next, add a score line to your canvas. You'll find this in the Design Panel, on the left, in the Shapes tab (it's the line in the upper left). Once the line appears on your canvas, make sure that the Operation is set to Score. Also change the height of the score line to 5.5″ and select Align > Center to your full card shape. I also changed the color of the card here so you can clearly see the score line in the center.

Now let's bring in the image that will spin on this card. This cake image seems to be the theme of the chapter so let's continue with it! Add the image to your canvas. Also, bring in a rectangle and size it to 4.25″ × 5.5″, then change this layer's operation to Guide. Align the guide to the right half of the card, which will make centering the cake image easier. You can send the guide layer to the back with the Arrange tool. Next, select the cake layer and the guide and then select Align > Center, making sure to leave a border to allow room for the offsets we will create in later steps.

PRO TIP

When choosing your focal image, make sure it is symmetrical. A design that is the same on both sides allows the spinning element to work its magic.

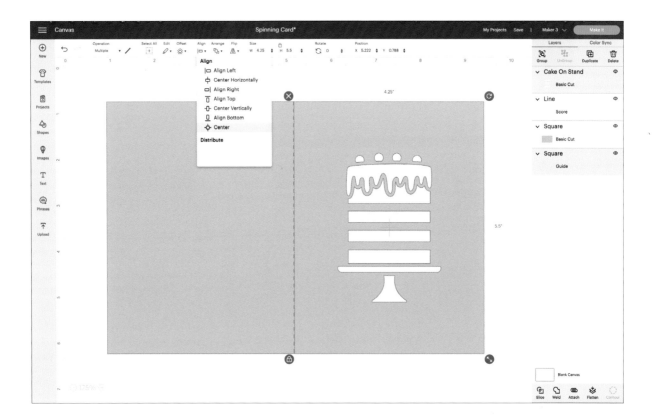

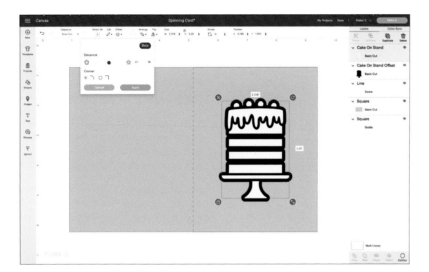

The next step is to create a narrow offset to the Cake on Stand image. An offset of 0.10˝ is good. With the offset layer now selected, add another offset. This time, make the offset a little larger: about 0.25˝ will work here. Your canvas should look similar to the images here.

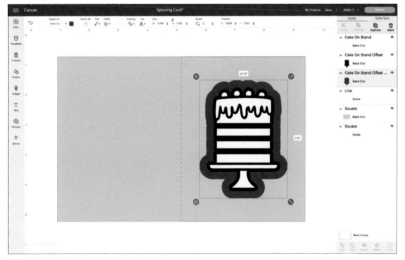

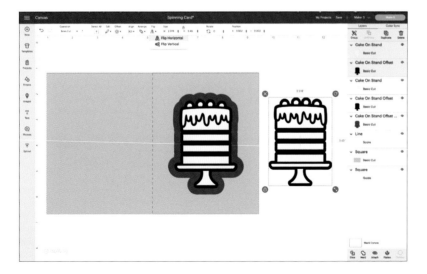

You now have the basic shapes of this card. Next, you will create the additional layers to complete this spinning card.

Select the original Cake on Stand layer and the smaller offset and then Duplicate them. Flip these two layers Horizontally, as shown here.

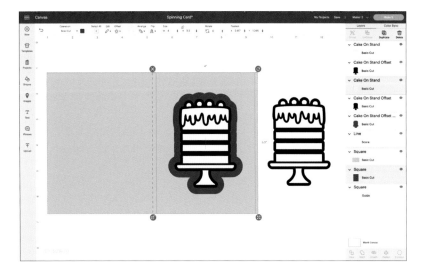

Add one more rectangle to the canvas, making this one 4″ × 5.5″: just slightly narrower than the final card will be. This will be used on the inside of the card (more on that in the Make It section). Before you move on to the next step, Arrange this new rectangle to be under your cake layer and all the offsets. Your canvas should look similar to the image here.

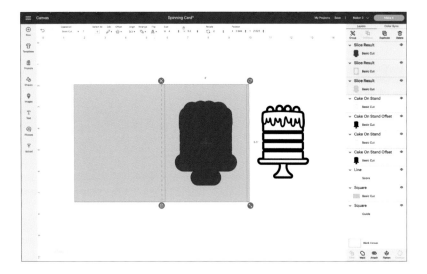

Now this is where the magic happens! Select the largest offset layer and the narrower rectangle, then Slice. You can see in the image here that there are now three Sliced layers. Delete one of the cake-shaped layers.

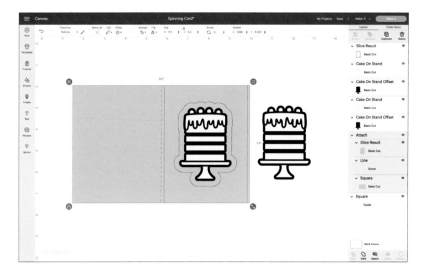

Select the other freshly sliced cake layer (sounds yummy!), the largest rectangle, and the score line and Attach. This will move all these layers to the top of your canvas, so you will need to Arrange and Send Backward until your cake and offset layer are at the top again, like the image here.

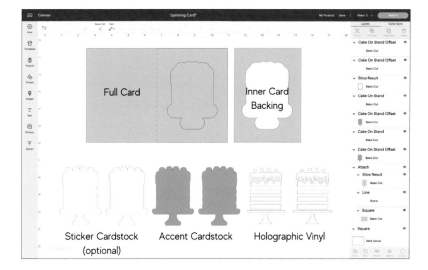

You may have noticed in the Materials list, there is mention of an optional sticker cardstock, which will make the spinning image sturdier and makes it easier to add the fishing line. These layers can also be made out of normal cardstock. Let's make these layers now by duplicating both of the smallest offset layers. Changing the layer colors will tell the machine that you'll be using a different material. If you will make them out of normal cardstock, it's best to keep all the cardstock layers the same color.

I've separated out all the layers in the image here and labeled them to make the assembly process clear for you. When all your elements are ready, click on the green Make It button and send your project to the mat.

MAKE IT

While your machine is cutting, stay close by because you'll need to change the settings for the various materials. After everything is cut, you'll start by assembling the spinning element, working from the inside out.

Grab your fishing line and your sticker cardstock or normal cardstock offset layers. Cut a piece of fishing line about 8″ long—you just need it to be a bit longer than your whole card when it's assembled. Lay the cardstock down sticky side up. If you are working with normal cardstock, apply a bead of glue down the center line. Now take the fishing line and lay it across the center, like the photo here.

If you're using glue, hold the fishing line tightly and keep it centered until the glue dries enough to secure the line. Next, add the other offset layer/sticker cardstock, making sure to line everything up.

Set this spinning contraption aside and begin to weed your vinyl by removing the unwanted parts, leaving only your cake image. Using transfer tape, apply your vinyl to your accent cardstock, then peel away the transfer tape. Repeat this process for the other matching vinyl and cardstock layers.

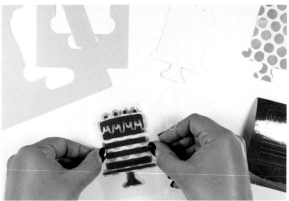

Apply glue to the back sides of these layers and adhere them to the matching sides of the cardstock attached to the fishing line.

Using a quick tack adhesive or glue runner, apply a strip across the top and bottom of the inner side of the full card, as shown here.

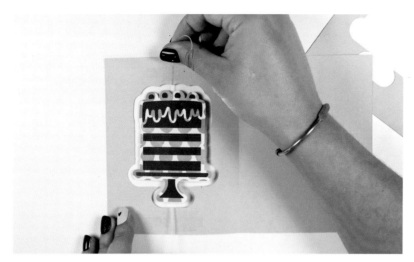

Next, stretch the fishing line across the inside of the card, making sure to center it. Apply more adhesive across the top, bottom, and all edges of the inner side of the full card, then adhere the inner-card backing to hide the string.

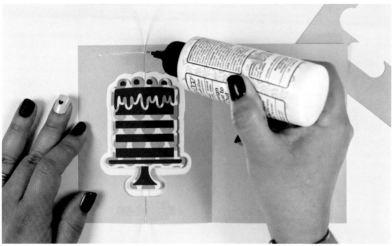

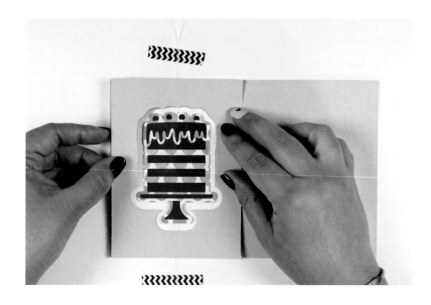

PRO TIP
Use washi or painter's tape to hold the fishing line tight during the assembly process.

Now for the final step. When all the glue is dry, trim the excess fishing line from the top and bottom of the card. Then, take it for a spin!

MAKE IT **EXTRA**

I hope this project has sparked all sorts of creative ideas for you! Although symmetrical images are the best when creating spinning cards, there are always workarounds. You could apply vinyl to a circle or square and have that be the spinning element. You could have multiple spinning elements on one card. The spinning piece can be vertical or horizontal. Truly, you could do so many things with a spinning card. I'd love to see what you create!

If you're looking for an envelope for your fantastic spinning card, flip on over to the Envelope project in this chapter for directions on how you can make a custom envelope that matches this sweet spinning card!

Envelope

The perfect addition to any handmade card is a handmade envelope! Your Cricut machine makes creating custom envelopes a quick and simple process. Of course, you can always add as many elements as you like. In this project we'll use the writing feature of your Cricut machine, which makes addressing and embellishing your envelopes fun and easy.

Materials

Cardstock
Cricut pen
Scraper tool
Glue/adhesive

Machine Compatibility

Any Cricut machine

Images Used

Cake on Stand #M2841CC1E
Envelope #M4131B

DESIGN IT

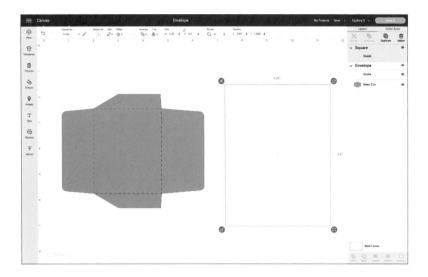

The first step is to add the Envelope image to your canvas. Cricut doesn't auto-matically know what size card you're working with, so you'll need to resize the Envelope image, making sure to keep the envelope layers grouped as you resize. To size your envelope to match your card, add a square or rectangle shape to your canvas and resize it to the same size as your card. Change that layer into a Guide, from the Opera-tion drop-down menu, like the image here.

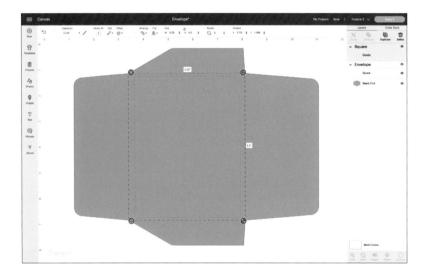

Using the Guide, resize the envelope so the guide has a small border within the inner rectangle of the Envelope image. Your canvas should be similar to what is shown here.

If you'd like to add text to your envelope, use the Filter option in the Text box and check the Writing box. This will give you all the options that will give you the best font results. Your Cricut machine writes by outlining the font unless the font is labeled as a Writing font. Keep that in mind when selecting your font.

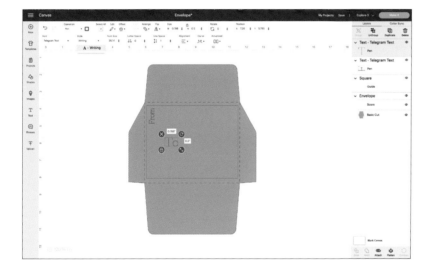

Size and rotate your text however you'd like it to be written on your envelope. Double-check that your text layers say Pen and choose your pen color.

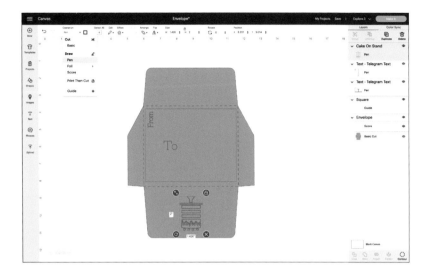

I will add this sweet little Cake on Stand image as a fun detail on the back of the envelope. Flip the image vertically and change the operation to Pen.

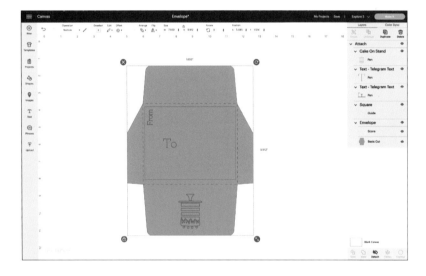

When all the layers are aligned and positioned the way you'd like them, select everything and Attach. Your final envelope should be similar to what you see here.

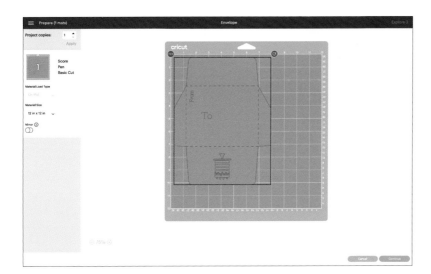

When you click on the green Make It button, your envelope should look just as it did on the canvas.

MAKE IT

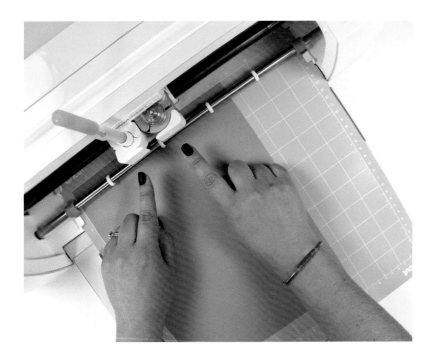

Choose your pen color and follow the prompts from Cricut Design Space.

If you're using a Cricut Maker, insert the pen into your machine on the left side of the carriage (A) and insert the Scoring Wheel on the right side (B).

If you're using a Cricut Explore machine, Design Space will prompt you to use a Scoring Tool and your pen in the left side of the carriage (A), and the Fine-Point Blade on the right side (B).

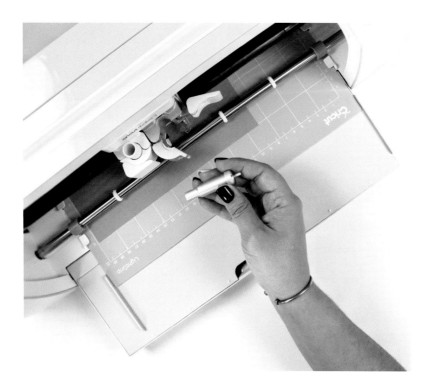

Following the prompts if using a Maker machine, when the writing and scoring is complete, swap out the Scoring Wheel for the Fine-Point Blade.

When your cuts are finished and your mat is unloaded, flip your mat over and roll it away from the cardstock, which will prevent the cardstock from curling.

Add any additional writing, coloring, or embellishments on your envelope and then fold along the score lines.

When gluing the sides, be aware of where the bottom flap ends. You don't need to apply glue along the entire side.

MAKE IT **EXTRA**

You can create your custom envelopes in a variety of sizes, as long as it stays within the maximum cut dimensions. Remember, when cutting on a mat, your Cricut can cut a maximum of 11.5″ wide and either 11.5″ or 23.5″ long, depending on your Cricut model and mat you're using. To make your envelope extra, you can add more text, a complete address, more drawn images, or you can cut images or shapes in the envelope for a peek-a-boo design. Another fun way to match your envelope to your card is by adding an insert; this can be used for party or wedding invitations and be done with your favorite elegant or patterned cardstock. Of course, you could always add stickers, washi tape, and/or glitter to your envelope. You can never go wrong with glitter!

CHAPTER FOUR

Let's Party

Parties are a great time to turn your Cricut on and craft your heart out!! In this chapter you'll learn how to create a festive paper banner, cake toppers, cupcake toppers, stickers for goodie bags, treat boxes, even how to create a stencil for a cake or other baked goods! While these projects are based around a bee theme, you can easily transform any of these items to your specific holiday or theme. There are a lot of tips and tricks within this chapter and I hope there is something that catches your crafty eye. Have fun celebrating your special occasion... or craft a party just because!

Paper Banner

Banners are always great decorations to accompany your party. They can easily be created to match any theme, color palette, or style. Paper banners can be created as your main decor or in addition to any other decorations you'd like to make for your celebration.

Materials Needed

Cardstock
Glue and/or adhesive foam dots
Twine/ribbon

Machine Compatibility

Maker or Explore series

Images Used

Honeycomb #M12AE763A
Two Bees with Heart #MBFDB01B

DESIGN IT

Start with a blank canvas and add your desired shape from the Shapes option on the far left of the screen (laptop/desktop) or from the bottom bar (portable device/tablet/phone). This will be the background shape for each letter in your banner. Some great options are triangles, rectangles, hearts, or even stars. For this banner I'll use a hexagon to tie in the bee theme. Size your shape accordingly, typically between 4″ and 8″ wide makes a great statement banner.

Once you have your shape selected and sized, add a circle to your canvas. Resize your circle to 1/8″ (0.125″) then Duplicate the circle.

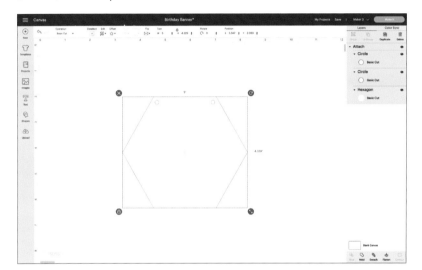

Position the circles on the two upper corners of your background shape. Use the Alignment tool to make sure your circles are positioned evenly. Select all three shapes and click on Attach. Your canvas should look like the image here.

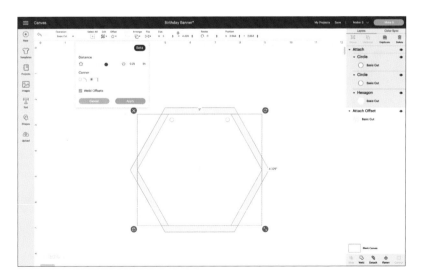

To give this banner some dimension, let's use the Offset tool. To do this, select the hexagon layer from your layers panel and then click Offset. The image here is using an offset of .25″. You can choose between rounded or sharp corners.

To make the next few steps easier, select everything you currently have on your canvas then click Group. Next, add Text to your canvas and type out your message. Select your favorite font and change the size of the text to fit inside the banner shape. Duplicate your background shape, one per letter. Your canvas and Layers panel should look similar to the image here. Here is where you can add additional images or details to personalize your project and make it extra special (see the "Make It Extra" section for ideas).

MAKE IT

Once your cardstock has been cut and removed from the mats, begin assembling by gluing your letters to your background shapes. A quick way to add dimension to your banner is by using adhesive foam dots (shown below).

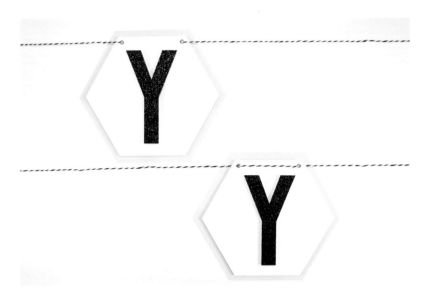

Finally, thread your twine through the holes, working from one side to the other. You can either thread through the front or the back depending on whether you'd like less or more twine exposed. Here is a visual for you to decide which suits your project better.

MAKE IT **EXTRA**

Adding flowers, pom-poms, textured paper, extra layers, or a dash of glitter can bring a little more fun to your party. For this banner bees and honeycomb were added to bring in some gold details and added interest.

Acetate Treat Box

Who doesn't love treats to take home from a party? Or better yet, a handmade treat box! This project can be customized in so many ways to match your party's theme. These little boxes also make a great addition to small holiday gatherings or just-because celebrations.

Materials Needed

Acetate
Scoring Tool or Scoring Wheel
Goodies and treats

Machine Compatibility

Maker or Explore series

Image Used

Hexagon Box #M54B6179

DESIGN IT

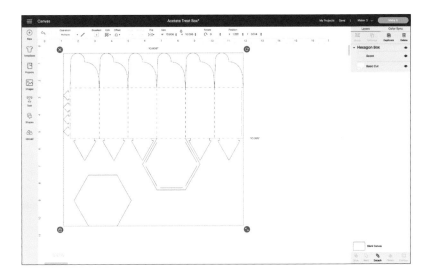

Cricut Design Space has a great variety of treat boxes to choose from. This image has all the cut and score lines in place. I resized the image to be a little larger (as shown here) to accommodate larger candies and to have room for extras.

MAKE IT

Most acetate has a protective liner on one side, so be sure to remove that before placing your material on your mat prior to cutting. When Design Space prompts you to select your material, click "Browse All Materials" and search for the Acetate setting. The green mat is the best mat to use for acetate. I also suggest using a brayer to roll over your acetate on the mat to remove any air bubbles.

Once cut and removed from the mat, fold along all of the score lines. Next, insert the small arrows into the slots on the opposite end (see the picture).

On the bottom of the box, insert the arrows into their respective slots to close the box. When all the arrows are tucked in place, take the other hexagonal piece, slide it into the bottom of the box, and lay it flat on the bottom. This will act as a protective layer so you don't poke your fingers when adding or removing candy from the box.

Once you've filled the box, fold over the top flaps to close the box. A dot of hot glue will keep these tabs closed.

MAKE IT **EXTRA**

Adding a bow on top of the box is a cute way to make this project a little more special. You can also add cardstock images to match your party decorations. These boxes can be filled with individually wrapped candy or would make great wedding favors filled with bulk candies.

Cake Stencil

If frosting and fondant isn't your thing but you'd still like to have a decorated cake, create a stencil and add some fun! You can also use this technique for a number of other homemade baked goods like pies, pancakes, and cookies.

Materials Needed

Cardstock or Kraft board

Food safe powder (e.g., cocoa, dehydrated berries, cinnamon, or powdered sugar)

Small sifter/strainer

Cake or other baked goods

Machine Compatibility

Maker or Explore series

Image Used

Hexagon Pattern #M33EA2

DESIGN IT

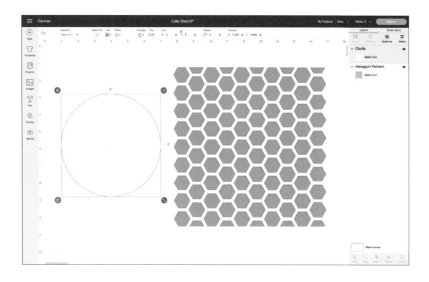

Start by measuring the cake you'd like to decorate. Keep in mind that the maximum width of the material Cricut machines can cut is 11.5″ wide, and you will need a border around your stencil. I'll be working with a small cheesecake that is 6″ in diameter.

Insert any decorative image or pattern you'd like on your cake. Some ideas are large shapes, basic letters in a stencil font, or patterns of shapes (like hearts). I'll be using a pattern of hexagons for this cake.

Add a shape on your canvas that matches the size of your cake. I'll start with a 6″ circle. Here's what my canvas looks like at this point.

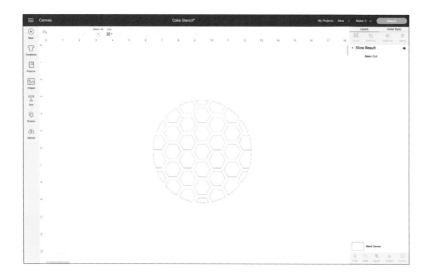

Once you have your image or pattern chosen, select that layer and the outline you created (the size of your cake). With both layers selected choose Align > Align to Center from the top Edit Bar. When your layers are centered, make sure they are both still selected and Slice. Next, remove the unwanted layers, leaving only the shapes you want to have cut from your material, as shown here.

MAKE IT

When you're on the Make It screen of Design Space you can select the image and drag it where you'd like it to cut. If you're cutting your stencil from a 12″ square piece of Kraft board or cardstock, drag your design to the center of the mat.

To remove your stencil from your mat, flip your mat upside down and slowly roll the mat away from your material, as shown in the image here. This prevents your material from curling.

When your material has been removed from the mat and any small pieces have been removed, place it gently on your cake. If your cake has frosting, hold the stencil above the cake when doing this step.

Now for the fun part! While the stencil is in place, gently sprinkle your powder through the sifter to cover the stencil. Sprinkle until the pattern is filled to your liking.

Gently pick up the stencil and set it to the side. Try not to shake any loose powder onto your freshly stenciled cake.

Your cake will look gorgeous all by itself or pair it with a matching themed cake topper as shown here. Happy celebrating!

MAKE IT **EXTRA**

To make it extra special, try creating layers of different images in different colors of powder. Using sprinkles instead of a sifted powder would also be a great way to add extra fun to your cake. This technique can also be used with powdered sugar on goodies like brownies or lemon bars. Have fun with this!

Cake Topper

A fun way to personalize your celebration is by adding a cake topper. These can be customized for any occasion or even just for fun. With cardstock and some creativity, you can easily create a whimsical cake topper.

Materials Needed

Cardstock
Glue and/or adhesive foam dots
Acrylic stick or wooden skewer

Machine Compatibility

Any Cricut machine (depending on the size desired)

Images Used

Honeycomb #M12AE763A
Two Bees With Heart #MBFDB01B

DESIGN IT

If this cake topper is the first decoration you'll be making for your party, start by adding your desired text and images to your canvas. I suggest creating an offset for your text to make it stand out.

PRO TIP

If you've already created other items for your party, you can copy and paste elements from one canvas to another. This is a great tool to use when creating multiple items with the same elements. I copied and pasted the elements above from a previous project in this chapter.

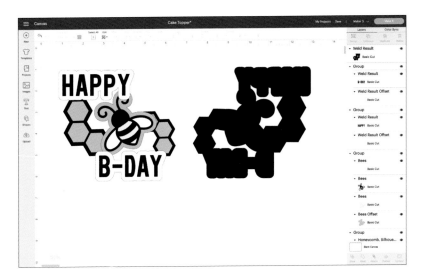

Once you have everything laid out where you'd like it, select everything and click on Duplicate. Then Weld all of those new duplicated layers together and then click on Flip > Horizontal in the top Edit Bar, as shown in the image here.

This reversed image will be the backing for your cake topper and it will also provide a guide when gluing all your pieces when assembling.

MAKE IT

Before gluing all of your pieces down, consider whether you'd like your acrylic stick or wooden skewer to be sandwiched in between the front and back layer or simply glued to the back, as shown here.

Then adhere your layers to your reversed base. I like to use a glue/tape runner for projects like these so the paper stays flat and doesn't wrinkle.

MAKE IT **EXTRA**

Adding additional layers and using adhesive foam dots/squares for added dimension are great ways to make it extra. Also, using cardstock that has texture, chrome, or glitter can add interest to your creation.

Another way to make your cake topper extra is by turning it into a Shaker Cake Topper. See the next project for detailed instructions.

Transparent Shaker Cake Topper

You've likely seen cake toppers before, maybe even shaker cake toppers, but have you seen a transparent shaker cake topper? This addition to your party will be a showstopper! Your guests and guest of honor will probably all want a turn shaking it, so be sure to follow the steps to get a great seal on your handmade shaker cake topper.

Materials Needed

Cardstock

Acetate

Glue

Glitter and/or shaker bits (beads/sequins)

Craft foam (with adhesive backing for best results)

Acrylic stick or wooden skewer

Knife Blade for Maker machine (best results) or Deep-Point Blade for Explore Air 2 machine

Machine Compatibility

Maker or Explore series

Images Used

Honeycomb #M12AE763A

Two Bees With Heart #MBFDB01B

DESIGN IT

Start with a blank canvas and add any text you'd like on your cake topper. When you have your text spaced the way you want it, Weld each word separately as this will make the next step easier. To make your text stand out, you can add an offset by selecting your welded words and using the Offset tool. Now select each word and its matching offset and Group together, like the image here.

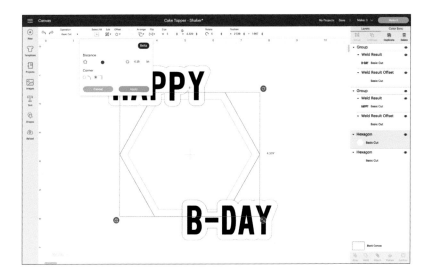

Next, add a main shape to your cake topper. When you have your shape the size you like, Duplicate the layer. This is where we start to build the frame of the shaker, select one of the main shapes and click the Offset tool again. This time instead of creating an offset on the outside, let's create an Inset by using −0.25 (negative .25″). Your canvas should appear similar to the image here.

PRO TIP

Change the colors of those larger shapes because these are going to be cut from acetate, a clear plastic material, which is going to make your shaker transparent and unique. I like to use a light-blue color for these layers (as shown above), but you can use whatever color you'd like as long as you remember what color each layer is going to be when it comes time for your cuts.

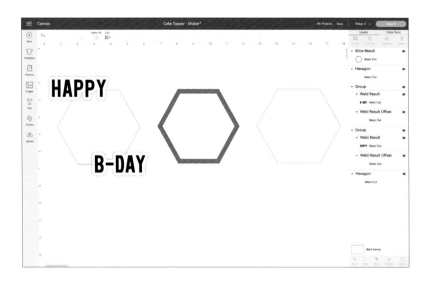

Next, Duplicate one of the larger shapes again and select the matching offset layer. Using the Alignment tool (located in the top Edit Bar), Center both layers, and then select Slice. Now, remove the two inner layers that were just created, keeping only the thin inset layer. Change the color so the machine knows this will be cut from a different material. This will be your foam layer, which creates the dimensional pocket for your shaker. Check the diagram here to see if your Design Space canvas looks similar.

PRO TIP

Use a craft foam that has an adhesive backing, as this will make the process much quicker than having to wait for glue to dry on both sides of the foam. It also eliminates any of your shaker elements from adhering to excess glue during the first half of the assembly process.

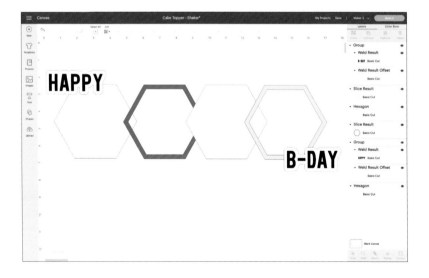

Working with that same layer, Duplicate the thin inset layer. Again, change the colors of this new layer because this is going to be a piece of accent cardstock you add to the outside of your shaker. You'll find more details on how to create the shaker sandwich/assembly in the following section. In the image here you will see what the basic layers look like. Your canvas should be similar.

Now that you have the main structure and text for your shaker, you can add any additional images and as many layers as you'd like.

MAKE IT

PRO TIP

Acetate can have a static charge to it. To reduce any static, you can gently swipe both sides of the acetate with a dryer sheet before or after cutting. You can also clean acetate with dish soap and water. Glitter and other small particles tend to stick to acetate, so this process will help cut back on that and will leave your shaker looking clean and professional.

I recommend using a brayer to remove air bubbles when placing your acetate material onto your mat. Most acetate has a protective plastic liner on one side, so be sure you remove the liner before applying your material to your mat.

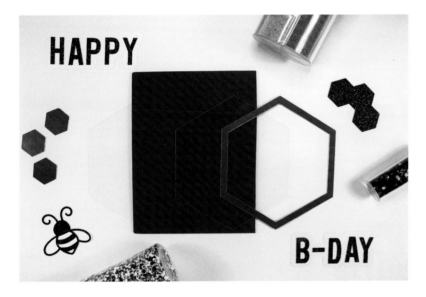

Now that you've got all of your layers cut, follow this order of assembly to create your shaker cake topper, starting from the bottom layer:

» Acetate – main shape
» Craft Foam – thin inset layer
» Glitter, beads, sequins, or other fun shakable items
» Acetate – main shape
» Cardstock – thin inset layer (to hide the foam and glue underneath)

Your text and any additional layers will then be glued on.

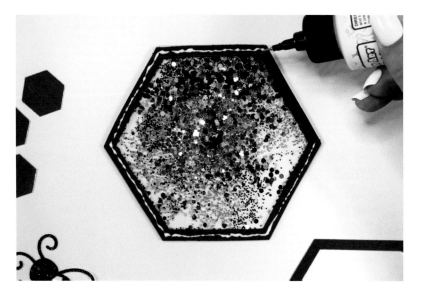

Once you have your foam attached to your acetate backing, fill it with glitter or other shaker bits. Along the foam edge apply a very thin bead of glue and then place the last piece of acetate on top. To ensure the glitter and shaker bits don't fall out, make sure there are no gaps once fully assembled.

The final steps are adding the accent cardstock as well as any additional elements you'd like to add to your shaker cake topper.

PRO TIP
A fine-tipped glue bottle is recommended for projects like these where you want to eliminate any pooling of adhesive. Important: Even though you'll be tempted to shake that shaker the moment you put it all together, allow the glue to dry first. Shaking it too soon is a mistake you don't want to make!

Once your shaker is dry, flip it over and glue your acrylic stick or wooden dowel to the center of your cake topper, about 2 inches up from the bottom (as shown in the image here).

MAKE IT **EXTRA**

Shaker cake toppers are already pretty extra but if you'd like to go even further, you can add more embellishments inside the shaker such as buttons, LED lights, or anything that is small enough to shake and add excitement. You can also add extra layers for more dimension. So many possibilities!

Cupcake Topper

Just like a cake topper but even cuter because they're smaller! These little additions to your cupcakes are a perfect way to add a touch more whimsy and fun to your party table. Cupcake toppers can easily be created in any style or theme.

Materials Needed

Cardstock
Glue/adhesive
Toothpick

Machine Compatibility

Any Cricut machine

Images Used

Honeycomb #M12AE763A
Two Bees With Heart #MBFDB01B

DESIGN IT

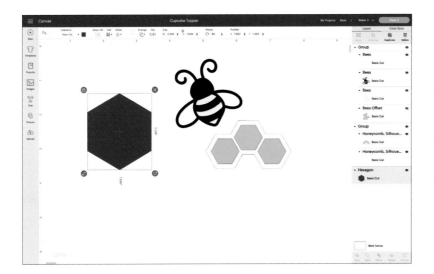

Start with a basic shape on your canvas, which will be your base. I'll use a hexagon. Then bring in some other images or shapes you'd like for your cake topper. Get creative with it! I copied and pasted some images I used for the other projects in this chapter, as shown here. Keep your cupcake toppers sized proportionately to your cupcakes, probably less than 3″ squared.

MAKE IT

After all your layers have been cut, assemble them onto the basic shape base. Build up the layers and have fun with it.

PRO TIP
It's helpful to use tweezers for handling tiny layers/ pieces of your cupcake topper.

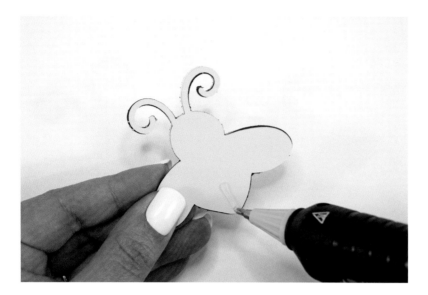

When your layers are all in place and any glue has dried, flip it over and add a small bead of glue, about 1″ long, to the back where you will glue on the toothpick. You can use hot glue for this part as it will be a quick set.

Quickly, while your glue is still tacky, add your toothpick. That's it!

MAKE IT **EXTRA**

Create multiple versions of cupcake toppers using different images to add variety to your party display. I added a rolled flower to this cupcake topper to add some dimension and color. Using different textures, colors, or specialty cardstock can make your cupcake toppers keepsakes.

Shaker Cupcake Topper

These little cupcake toppers are just as fun to make as they are to shake! Fair warning: There could be some fighting over who gets the cupcake with the shaker on top, so you might want to make a few.

Materials Needed

Cardstock

Acetate

Glue

Glitter and/or shaker bits (beads/sequins)

Craft foam (with adhesive backing for best results)

Toothpick

Knife Blade for Maker machine (best results) or Deep-Point Blade for Explore Air 2 machine

Machine Compatibility

Maker or Explore series

Image Used

Two Bees With Heart #MBFDB01B

DESIGN IT

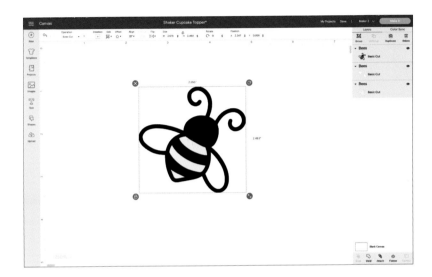

Begin by adding your main image to your canvas. I recommend using an image that has several cuts as this will create pockets for you to add glitter and other shaker bits. I'll use this cute little bee to match the rest of the decorations for this party. The image here has several layers to it, which is the type of image that will work best.

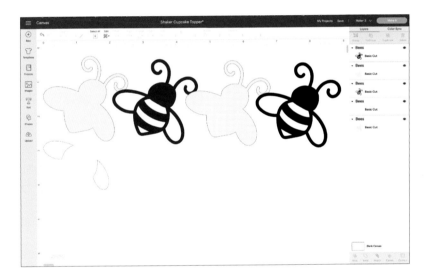

From these layers we will create the pockets for the shaker. The easy way to do this is to duplicate the base and top layers. Change the colors of these new layers as shown here. These layers will be used with the following materials:

» Cardstock (yellow and white) base layer
» Foam (dark gray) this layer will create the pocket
» Acetate (light blue) this layer will seal in your shaker bits
» Cardstock (black) final layer to conceal any glue/foam layers underneath

MAKE IT

When cutting your foam, use the Knife Blade and a green or purple mat, which will give you the cleanest cut possible. I like to use foam that has an adhesive backing to make the assembly process clean and easy. Once cut, apply the foam layer to your base cardstock, as shown here.

Now that you have little pockets to fill, go ahead and add your glitter, beads, sequins or whatever else you'd like to make your cupcake topper shake. Once filled, use a fine line of glue and attach your acetate, followed by your final cardstock layers.

After all your glue is completely dry, flip it over to glue on the toothpick. Do not flip over your cupcake topper before it's dry.

MAKE IT EXTRA

Shaker cupcake toppers may already be a little "extra," but you can make these as elaborate as you like. Adding extra layers or using different shaker bits can really make these cupcake toppers fun! After using them as cupcake toppers, you can clean the toothpicks and use them as straw inserts—just for fun—or to identify whose cup/straw is whose.

Stickers for Goodie Bags

Goodie bags are always a good idea for a party! Make them even sweeter with a personalized touch. Add stickers to match your theme and customize them to thank your guests for coming to your celebration.

Materials Needed

Sticker paper
Printer
Acetate goodie bags
Goodies to fill bags

Machine Compatibility

Maker or Explore series

Image Used

Bumble Bee #MD86F22

DESIGN IT

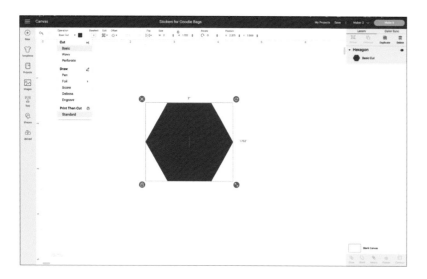

Bring your desired basic sticker shape onto your canvas. I chose a hexagon for these stickers. To achieve this look with a printed background, you can either upload your own background image (see page xi in the Introduction chapter for details) or you can use a pattern within Design Space. To use a pattern, select your shape and find the option that says Basic Cut and then change that to Print Then Cut Standard.

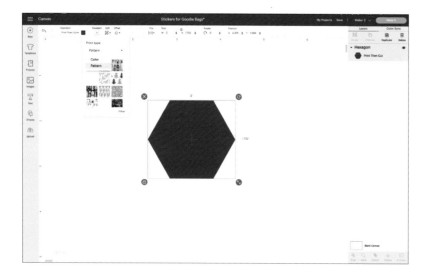

Next, click the dark-gray box next to where it now says Print Then Cut and select Pattern from the drop-down menu. Here you can select any patterns you'd like. When you upload your own patterns they will be shown here.

Once you have your selected pattern, you can start to fill in your shape with text and images. When everything is the way you like it, select all the layers and Flatten. This will combine all your layers into one print layer and your Cricut will cut around the basic shape. Your canvas and Layers panel should look like the example here.

PRO TIP

To maximize your Print Then Cut area, bring a rectangle onto the canvas and click the lock icon in the corner to unlock the proportions so you can size it to 6.75″ x 9.25″. Select this rectangle and then select Arrange from your options and Send to Back. From here you will duplicate your flattened sticker as many times as necessary to arrange into this rectangle. Here's an example of what the Design Space canvas looked like for this project.

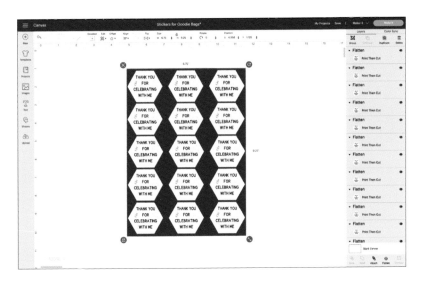

When everything is arranged as you like it, hide or delete the background rectangle. Then select all of your stickers and click on Attach. This will keep everything where you have it when you cut your stickers.

MAKE IT

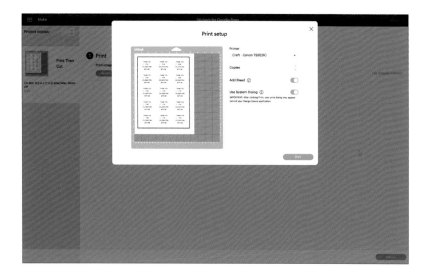

Now comes the techy part. When you click Make It you will be prompted to Send to Printer. I always prefer to use System Dialog, which allows me to fine-tune the printing job for my particular printer (sometimes this box pops up behind Design Space). I like to use the rear tray of my printer when printing on materials other than copy paper.

When your stickers have completed printing and have dried for a few minutes, place your sticker sheet on the upper-left corner of your mat. I always like to use a brayer to make sure there are no air bubbles between the mat and material.

Each sticker sheet has a different thickness so you may want to try using different cut settings for your particular material. I like to use the Iron-On setting if my sticker sheet is thin and I want my stickers to remain on the backing. If I want my stickers to cut all the way through, I will use the Cardstock setting. Again, try small test cuts before you cut the whole sheet just to be sure.

When cut correctly, your stickers will peel off easily.

Now your bags are ready to be filled with goodies and then sealed with your custom stickers.

MAKE IT **EXTRA**

A fun way to make your stickers extra special is to add laminate overlays. You can find a variety of holographic overlays that you can add to your sticker sheets before cutting; just make sure to keep the overlay within the black box (registration marks) once printed. Also, if using any sort of laminate, you'll need to adjust your cut settings to allow for this added thickness. When using a laminate overlay, I like to cut using the Heavy Cardstock setting. I definitely recommend test cuts when using new materials.

Now that you know how to make stickers, you can create stickers for every occasion or purpose. There are so many different types of sticker paper that you can get really creative with making planner stickers, birthday stickers, stickers for custom cards, stickers for your car, address labels, and so on. The possibilities are nearly endless! You can even use these instructions and techniques to create custom tattoos using printable tattoo paper.

Conclusion

This book was written as "the book I wish I had when I started using a Cricut." Each project has been designed with the intention that you could pick up this book and create a beautiful work of heart no matter your skill level or experience. The "Pro Tips" found throughout these pages come from my own trials and errors of crafting. My goal is to share with you the things I have learned along the way.

I'd love to see what you create, so feel free to tag me on social media or strike up a conversation with me on Instagram @lovebird_heartworks or other social media channels at Lovebird Heartworks. Let's talk craft!

Acknowledgements

This is the hardest part of the book to write. I'm incredibly excited, scared, and joyful, yet writing this with a face of bittersweet tears. I want to thank God, who put the vision of Lovebird Heartworks together! What began as painting live during rock concerts has morphed into a platform that I'm now able to share not only crafting, but also love—it's what started all of this. I'm beyond grateful for both of my parents, Paul and Marianne, who always fostered my creativity and exploration into new artistic mediums. My dad, the best Papa ever, still encourages me to this day. Even right now, telling me that the way he sees it, "This is God's book and (I am) the instrument for all the readers to access their passion and creativity!" Thank you, Daddy. I sure do wish I could share this book with my mama, she passed away in 2012 after a two-year battle with pancreatic cancer. She never got to see me live the life she had hoped and prayed for, a life where I get to teach and create, but I know she knows, and I get little nods every now and then when I feel her presence. Love your show, Mama, always!

My two brothers and I were so blessed by our parents, and all grew up to be differently creative. My younger brother, Michael, is an amazing musician and has such a unique sound and perspective on the world—always has! Thank you for always having my back and being so encouraging when it comes to living out this dream, love you Bubs! My older brother, Patrick, was an incredible photographer and had a beautiful way of seeing the world in a way that others just don't. He passed unexpectedly in 2020 due to diabetic complications. I remember the last conversation we had just days before he passed, he was telling me he was so proud of what I was creating, not just artistically, but also the family I was creating. I miss his wisdom and peanut gallery comments more than I can say. Hold fast, Patches!

This book would be an unrealized dream if it weren't for my husband, Steve. Thank you for stepping up and holding down the fort—all the while encouraging me and creating a space for me to be able to flow creatively at all hours of the day and night. Thank you for believing in me, I love you, Stevie! Steve gave me my first Cricut and kickstarted this whole technically creative side of me that I never knew was even a possibility! I can only hope that my two children, Elbee and Carver, know how much I appreciate their love notes of encouragement and how much joy they bring me. You two keep me going—I pray that you follow your dreams and aren't afraid to put it all out there and show up authentically with your whole hearts!

To all my family and friends—your support and encouragement mean more than I can express! Thank you for understanding and still loving me while I fell off the face of the planet and crafted like a tornado to create this book. Speaking of, to Kelly Reed and the team at Rocky Nook, thank you! Thank you for inviting me to create and share this book and making this entire experience a reality!

Thank you to the friends I've haven't met face to face (yet) but have become so close with over the years on social media as we share our creative projects, inspirations, and support for one another in this crafting community!

When I was little I always wanted to "be an art teacher." Well, this is my version of that—and it wouldn't be possible without YOU! Thank you, I love you!

About the Author

Megan Meketa's passion for crafting goes as far back as she can remember. As a young girl she loved to make cards and color with her mom. That creativity stayed with her as she now crafts with her own children, teaching them a tangible way to show love to others with handmade notes and gifts. Following her heart, creating, and sharing has provided Megan with opportunities to collaborate with Michaels, Cricut, B-Flex America, Speedball, Pinterest, and more. Megan was also featured in the Cricut product release commercial for Infusible Ink.

Megan spreads love and creativity through her business, Lovebird Heartworks. You can connect with her on Instagram @lovebird_heartworks, other social media channels at Lovebird Heartworks, or visit www.LovebirdHeartworks.com for more works of heart.